What the Cults Believe

Second Edition, Revised

By

IRVINE ROBERTSON

Pickering & Inglis
LONDON · GLASGOW

To my beloved and our stalwart four

Contents

Preface

THIS REVISION contains the salient features of the cults, as did the first writing. However, the format is different, and much material has been added. Today we do not speak of "the four major cults"—as if the field of cultism were so limited. Certainly the Worldwide Church of God, the Unification Church, and more recently The Way International have come into places of considerable influence. Christian Science does not appear to have maintained its position of major outreach. There remains a growing difference of opinion among evangelical scholars as to the inclusion of Seventh Day Adventism as a cult alongside such movements as Mormonism and Jehovah's Witnesses. Seventh Day Adventism adheres to the main fundamental doctrines of the orthodox Christian faith. Yet there are distinctives that are deviate. Major among those distinctives, and unique to Seventh Day Adventism, is the doctrine of investigative judgment. It is also called "the cleansing of the sanctuary." This unusual interpretation of Scripture is considered in some detail in this book.

It is estimated that there are as many as three thousand cults active on the North American continent. The founders of "Christian cults" usually claim revelation from above which either reinterprets the Bible or reestablishes teaching lost since the days of "the early church." Other movements are many, and cater to the desire for the mysterious, the mystical. Usually rooted in Hindu philosophy, they tend to be eclectic, seeking to add to the Christian faith rather than to replace it. Their influence is widespread, both within and without the boundaries of Protestantism. A new section has been included in this revision. It deals with the fundamental teachings of Eastern mysticism. Major movements and their distinctives are considered, albeit the source and basics are really the same for all of them.

Introduction

"Now THE SPIRIT speaketh expressly, that in the latter times some shall depart from the faith, giving heed to seducing spirits, and doctrines of devils; speaking lies in hypocrisy" (1 Tim. 4:1-2a).

Current methods of the attack upon truth fall into two main classifications. The first is an appeal to pride through rationalistic philosophy. The second demands a credulity that is akin to superstition, and calls it "faith." A common feature is the denial, in whole or in part, of the deity of Jesus Christ. "This is that spirit of antichrist [which is], in the world" (1 John 4:3). It impugns both Christ's person and His work. As Samuel Zwemer once said about Islam, "It gives Him a place by displacing Him."

The "Christian" cult ostensibly accepts the authority of the Bible. But it is the Bible subject to misinterpretation. Generally, the cultist is well acquainted with key passages in the Scriptures. His arguments are well spiced with proof texts by which he displays his knowledge of the Bible. He impresses the less-informed individual.

The purpose of this book is not to foster argument or debate, nor to provide information merely for rebuttal. Because to be forewarned is to be forearmed, the salient features and distinctive doctrines of current cults are presented to inspire orthodox believers to a positive yet loving offensive in meeting false teaching. Few details are given in this volume concerning the personal lives of the founders of the cults. Other sources provide ample information concerning the eccentricities and reportedly dishonest activities of Joseph Smith, Charles Taze Russell, et al. It should be noted that little is gained by attack on the characters of these men. Resentful denial is the usual response to such, and an extra barrier may be erected between the Christian witness and the cultist he seeks to win. It is the Truth that makes men free. The best method to use is simply that of presenting the Truth and of giving a positive personal testimony of what God has done.

It should be remembered that proof texts are not disproved by other proof texts. However, a knowledge of the texts used by the cultist within the immediate and remote contexts will often provide the means by which the conversation may be steered into positive channels. The exaltation of the Lord Jesus Christ is indispensable in witnessing. Essential are knowledge of the Word, conscious dependence on the Holy Spirit, and love for those who are deluded.

Major Doctrines of Orthodox Christianity

THE SOURCE OF AUTHORITY

A COMPOSITE doctrinal statement from evangelical sources would include the declaration that the Bible, consisting of the sixty-six books of the Old and New Testaments, is a divine revelation, of which the original manuscripts were verbally inspired by the Holy Spirit. The Bible is absolute in its authority, complete in its revelation, final in its content, and without any errors in its statements. In the Bible is contained all that is necessary for the service of God and for our salvation. It is therefore the supreme and final authority in all matters of faith and conduct, and is the only rule and norm by which all teaching is to be judged. (See Isa. 8:19-20; Luke 16:29-31; Gal. 1:8-9; 2 Tim. 3:15-17; and 2 Peter 1:21.)

THE DOCTRINE OF GOD

The belief of traditional Christianity is given in the *Westminster Shorter Catechism* (Question 6): "There are three persons in the Godhead; the Father, the Son, and the Holy Ghost; and these three are one God, the same in substance, equal in power and glory." (See Deut. 6:4; Jer. 10:10; Matt. 3:16-17; 28:19; and 2 Cor. 13:14.)

THE DOCTRINE OF JESUS CHRIST

Most important in the message of the gospel are the person and work of our Lord Jesus Christ. "What think ye of Christ?" (Matt. 22:42). The answer to that question will frequently indicate veracity or heresy in any system that allies itself with Christianity.

13

Jesus Christ is the image of the invisible God, perfect in Godhood and perfect in manhood. One with the Father from eternity, He took upon Himself the nature of man, and was conceived by the Holy Ghost and born of the virgin Mary. Having died on the cross as a substitutionary sacrifice for sin, He rose from the dead in the same body that was laid to rest in the tomb. He ascended into heaven in that glorified body, and is now there interceding in behalf of all who believe in Him. He will come again, personally, bodily, and visibly, to judge the living and the dead, and to set up His Kingdom. (See Matt. 1:18-25; Luke 24; Acts 2:31-36; Phil. 2:5-8; Col. 1:15-18; 1 Thess. 4:16-18; Heb. 4:14-16; 1 Pet. 2:24-25; Rev. 11:15-17; 20:4-6, 11-15.)

THE DOCTRINE OF MAN

After God had made all other creatures, He created man, male and female. He formed the body of the man of the dust of the ground, and the woman from a rib of the man. He endued them with living, reasonable, and immortal souls. Made after God's own image, in knowledge, righteousness, and holiness, they had the law of God written in their hearts, with power to fulfill it, yet they were subject to fall. They were given dominion over the fish of the sea, the birds of the air, and every living creature on earth.

Our first parents, being left to the freedom of their own will, fell from the estate wherein they were created, by sinning against God (Gen. 3:6-13; 2 Cor. 11:3). All mankind, descending from Adam by ordinary generation, sinned in him, and fell with him in his first transgression (Gen. 2:17; Acts 17:26; Rom. 5:12-20; 1 Cor. 15:21-22). Thus all mankind, having lost communion with God, are under His wrath and curse, and so are made liable to all miseries in this life, to death itself, and to the pains of hell forever (Rom. 5:14; 6:23; Eph. 2:3).

At death, the souls of the believers enter into the presence of Christ (Luke 23:43; John 14:3; 2 Cor. 5:1-8; Phil. 1:23); the souls of the wicked are in immediate torment (Luke 16:22-23; 2 Pet. 2:9); while bodies rest in the grave until the time of the resurrections (Rom. 8:23; 1 Thess. 4:14-18). There will be a resurrection of the just unto life, and of the wicked unto eternal damnation (John 5:28-29; 1 Thess. 4:14-18; Rev. 20:4-15).

THE DOCTRINE OF SALVATION, OR THE ATONEMENT

Salvation is by grace, a gift of God, through faith in the Lord Jesus Christ. He died a voluntary death upon the cross as a substitutionary sacrifice for sin (1 Cor. 15:3; 1 Peter 2:23-24). Those who receive Christ by faith have their sins forgiven (Eph. 1:7); are born of the Spirit, thus becoming children of God (John 1:12-13); and are made new creatures in Christ Jesus (2 Cor. 5:17).

THE DOCTRINE OF ESCHATOLOGY, OR THINGS TO COME

Jesus Christ will come again personally, bodily, and visibly. At His appearance, the dead in Christ will rise first. Together with the living saints, they will be changed and caught up to meet the Lord "in the air." This is known as the rapture of the saints (1 Thess. 4:16-17; see also 1 Cor. 15:51-58). The Great Tribulation follows (the seventieth week of Daniel 9), and ends with the appearance of the Lord with His saints for judgment of peoples on earth (the revelation of Jesus Christ). Thereafter, He will set up His Kingdom, which will endure for 1,000 years (the Millennium).[1] During this period Satan will be bound, and there

---

1. This is the pre-Tribulation position. It is recognized that numerous orthodox, evangelical Christians hold that the second coming of Christ is altogether subsequent to the Tribulation period. Their position, known as the post-Tribulation position, maintains that both the rapture of the church and the revelation of Christ in person to set up His Kingdom occur in swift succession *after* the Tribulation.

will be universal peace and prevailing righteousness on earth. At the end of the millennial reign of Christ, Satan will be released for a short time, will wage final war against the Lord, and will be cast with his cohorts into the eternal lake of fire. There will be a resurrection of the wicked (the second resurrection), and the judgment of the great white throne will follow. All whose names are not found in the Lamb's book of life will be cast into the lake of fire for eternal punishment. (See Matt. 24:29-30; 26:64; Acts 1:11; 1 Thess. 4:16; 2 Thess. 2:7-8; and Rev. 1:7; 20:1-6, 11-15.) The saints will spend eternity with the Lord.

1

Mormonism

THE CHURCH OF JESUS CHRIST OF LATTER-DAY SAINTS (whose members have been nicknamed Mormons) claims to be the restoration of the true church established by Jesus Christ. It has no association in any way with Roman Catholicism or with Protestantism. "Its theology, its organization, and its practices are in many respects entirely unique among today's Christian denominations."[1] "It possesses the divine priesthood of God, . . . and is headed by prophets and Apostles as was the Church in the days of Peter and Paul."[2] Indeed, "if it had not been for Joseph Smith and the restoration, there would be no salvation. There is no salvation outside The Church of Jesus Christ of Latter-day Saints."[3]

In numerous publications it is emphasized that the church which had been established by Jesus Christ became corrupt. Apostasy triumphed and divinely appointed authority ceased. The church "drifted without direction" after the death of the apostle John. There was no revelation, authority, or divinely approved ministry until the true church was restored through the prophet Joseph Smith.

Born in Sharon, Vermont, in 1805, Smith had moved to Palmyra, New York. There, in 1820, he reported seeing

1. Gordon B. Hinckley, *What of the Mormons?* (Salt Lake City: Deseret News Press, n.d.), p. 2.
2. Mark E. Peterson, *Which Church Is Right?* (Salt Lake City: Deseret News Press, n.d.), p. 25.
3. Bruce R. McConkie, *Mormon Doctrine* (Bookcraft, Salt Lake City, 1966), p. 670 (hereafter cited as McConkie).

his first heavenly vision. Two personages appeared. Their "brightness and glory defy all description. . . . One of them spake unto me, calling me by name and said, pointing to the other—*This is My Beloved Son. Hear Him!*"[4]

There followed a series of visitations from a "resurrected personage" named Moroni. These visitations culminated on Sept. 22, 1827. Moroni delivered to Smith the "golden plates," the translation of which is known as the Book of Mormon. In May 1829, John the Baptist appeared and ordained Smith along with Oliver Cowdery to the Aaronic priesthood. In June of that same year, Peter, James, and John "came to Joseph Smith and Oliver Cowdery and conferred upon them the Melchizedek Priesthood" (McConkie 478). This established the authority of the "Church," for without the "Melchizedek Priesthood" "salvation in the kingdom of God" is not "available for men on earth" (McConkie 479).

On April 6, 1830, The Church of Jesus Christ of Latter-day Saints was formally established in Fayette, New York, with six members. It has grown to a present membership of more than three million, with branches in every state of the Union and more than a score of foreign lands. Various estimates cite as many as fourteen thousand missionaries in active ministry, with some six thousand serving part-time. Full-time missionaries serve voluntarily, without pay, normally for a period of two years. The majority are young men between the ages of nineteen and twenty-five.

4. P Joseph Smith 2:17. The Mormon sacred books are cited in the following ways in this book: The Book of Mormon and the Pearl of Great Price are each composed of individual books, the same basic format as is found in the Bible. References to the individual books begin either with the abbreviation BM (for the Book of Mormon) or with P (for the Pearl of Great Price) and are followed by the title of the individual book, the chapter number, and the verse number— BM 2 Nephi 29:6 and P Joseph Smith 2:35, for example. Doctrine and Covenants is divided into sections. References to individual sections begin with the abbreviation D&C, which is followed by the section number and the verse number—D&C 27:1, for example. The three books are published by The Church of Jesus Christ of Latter-day Saints at Salt Lake City, Utah.

THE SOURCES OF AUTHORITY

We believe the Bible to be the word of God as far as it is translated correctly; we also believe the Book of Mormon to be the word of God.

We believe all that God has revealed, all that He does now reveal, and we believe that He will yet reveal many great and important things pertaining to the Kingdom of God [P Articles of Faith 8-9].

It is strongly emphasized that the canon of Scripture has never been closed. God's direction has always been by personal communication through commissioned servants. God's laws in one period have been repealed in others, "when a more advanced stage of the divine plan had been reached."[5] Thus in the Sermon on the Mount (see Matt. 5:17-18), the Savior, it is taught, repealed the Law of Moses. Current and continued revelations are held to be essential characteristics of the church in order that the officers might teach with authority. The president of the church, in particular, is "like unto Moses—"a seer, a revelator, a translator, and a prophet, having all the gifts of God which he bestows upon the head of the church" (D&C 107:91-92). He speaks, upon occasion, with as much authority as does the Bible, or as any other of the accepted sacred books, the Book of Mormon, the Doctrine and Covenants, and the Pearl of Great Price.

A. The official version of the Bible used by the Mormon Church is the King James Version. A revision by Joseph Smith, called the Inspired Version, was not completed and is not used by the Salt Lake City group. It should be noted that to the Mormon the Bible is not absolute in authority, and neither final nor complete in its revelation. The qualifying clause "as far as it is translated correctly" suggests

5. James E. Talmage, *A Study of the Articles of Faith* (Salt Lake City: The Church of Jesus Christ of Latter-day Saints, 1961), p. 303 (hereafter cited as Talmage).

errors in translation which presumably have been corrected by subsequent revelations.

B. The Book of Mormon "is a divinely inspired record, made by the prophets of the ancient peoples who inhabited the American continent for centuries before and after the time of Christ" (Talmage 255). It "contains a record of . . . the fulness of the gospel" (D&C 20:9; see also 42:12, etc.). The prophet himself declared that "the Book of Mormon was the most correct of any book on earth, and the keystone of our religion" (McConkie 99, quoting Joseph Smith).

It tells the epic story of two waves of immigration to the American continent. In the first, the Jaredite nation "followed their leader from the Tower of Babel at the time of the confusion of tongues" (Talmage 260) about 2,250 B.C. These people flourished until 590 B.C., when internal warfare led to their total destruction. The final battle took place at the hill Cumorah, near the present Palmyra, New York. The second migration was under Lehi, of the tribe of Manasseh, about the year 600 B.C. Two nations, the Nephite and the Lamanite, came from Lehi's sons Nephi and Laman. The former "advanced in the arts of civilization, built large cities, and established prosperous commonwealths" (Talmage 260). The latter "fell under the curse of divine displeasure; they became dark in skin . . . and degenerated into the fallen state in which the American Indians—their lineal descendants—were found . . . in later times" (Talmage 260). The final struggle between these two nations also ended at Cumorah, about A.D. 421. The last Nephite survivor, Moroni, completed the Book of Mormon on the golden plates and hid them in the hill Cumorah. He later appeared, a resurrected being, in 1823-27 and gave the plates to Joseph Smith for translation.

The plates were inscribed in characters called "reformed Egyptian" (BM Mormon 9:32). To enable translation,

Smith was given the "Urim and Thummim." Perhaps resembling a pair of eyeglasses, these were "two stones in silver bows—and these stones [were] fastened to a breastplate" (P Joseph Smith 2:35). With the aid of these, he completed the translation between December 1827 and February 1828. The story is told in the "Writings of Joseph Smith," which is found in the Pearl of Great Price. In "Writings of Joseph Smith" 2:63-65, Smith cited Professor Charles Anthon as certifying the authenticity of the "reformed Egyptian characters." Anthon vehemently denied this, branding the whole story as "perfectly false." In published statements, the Smithsonian Institution denied knowledge of any authentic cases of ancient Hebrew or Egyptian writing having been found in the New World.[6]

Nevertheless, it is declared that "almost all of the doctrines of the gospel are taught in the Book of Mormon with much greater clarity and perfection than . . . in the Bible. Anyone . . . will find conclusive proof of the superiority of the Book of Mormon teachings" (McConkie 99).

Apparently, Mormon missionaries make much of the claim that the prophet Ezekiel spoke of two books, using the imagery of "two sticks" (Ezek. 37:16-17). The Bible, they say, is the stick of Judah. The Book of Mormon is the stick of Ephraim and records God's dealings with a portion of the tribe of Joseph. It is "now in the hands of church members who nearly all are of Ephraim" (McConkie 767; see also D&C 27:5).

In truth, the word translated "stick" literally means "tree, wood, or pole." The "stick" is the emblem of the royal scepter. Thus it is that the "stick of Judah" represents the Southern Kingdom; the "stick of Joseph" is the Northern Kingdom, of which the first king was Jeroboam, of the

6. For further details concerning the genuineness of the Book of Mormon, see Gordon R. Lewis, *Confronting the Cults* (Nutley, N.J.: Presby & Ref., 1966), pp. 52 ff.

tribe of Ephraim. Ezekiel the prophet was predicting the restoration and future union of the two kingdoms.

C. Doctrine and Covenants is composed of 136 sections, of which all but two are "revelations given to Joseph Smith, the Prophet" (title page). Section 135 tells of his martyrdom, and 136 is "The Word and Will of the Lord, given through President Brigham Young." An official declaration prohibiting polygamy was appended in 1890 by President Wilford Woodruff.

Significant revelations in this book pertain to baptism for the dead (sections 124, 127-28), celestial marriage (section 132:19c-20), and plural marriage (section 132). In contrast, 42:22-23 and 49:15-16 seem to command monogamy! The Book of Mormon says nothing about the first two matters, and strongly denounces polygamy (Jacob 2: 23-36).

D. The Pearl of Great Price is a small volume containing "a selection from the revelations, translations, and narrations of Joseph Smith" (title page). It is usually bound with the Doctrine and Covenants. The Thirteen Articles of Faith are also included.

THE DOCTRINE OF GOD

"We believe in God the Eternal Father, and in His Son Jesus Christ, and in the Holy Ghost" (P Articles of Faith, 1).

The Book of Mormon seems to equate the Mormon concept of the Trinity with that of orthodox Christianity: "This is the doctrine of Christ, and the only and true doctrine of the Father, and of the Son, and of the Holy Ghost, which is one God, without end" (BM 2 Nephi 31:21; see also Alma 11:44, etc.). The theologian Talmage, however, explains that "three personages composing the great presiding council of the universe have revealed themselves to man. . . . These three are separate individuals, physically distinct from each other" (Talmage 39). Refuting the *Westminster Shorter Catechism,* which states that "there are three persons in the Godhead; the Father, the Son, and the Holy Ghost; and these three are one God, the same in substance, equal in power and glory" (Question 6), Talmage declares that this "cannot rationally be construed to mean that the Father, the Son, and the Holy Ghost are one in substance and in person" (Talmage 40). The oneness of the Godhead, it is declared, "implies no mystical union of substance, nor any unnatural and therefore impossible blending of personality" (Talmage 41). McConkie puts it plainly: "There are three *Gods* . . . separate in personality, . . . united as one in purpose, in plan, and in all the attributes of perfection" (McConkie 317). The plural word *Elohim* is used as the exalted name, the title of God, the Eternal Father.

A. God is "an organized being just as we are, who are now in the flesh."[7] This is in keeping with the doctrine that God is a "progressive being, . . . his perfection possesses . . . the capacity of eternal increase" (Talmage 529). He "was perhaps once a child, and mortal like we ourselves, and rose step by step in the scale of progress."[8] Involved in the scheme of eternal progression, He is simply far, far ahead of us, His children. It is reiterated that "as man is, God once was; as God is, man may become."[9] Thus it is taught that Abraham and Isaac and Jacob "have entered into their exaltation and are not angels, but are gods" (D&C 132:37). It remained for Brigham Young to confuse things somewhat by adding, "Adam is our father and god, the only God with whom we have to do."[10]

7. Joseph F. Smith, *Gospel Doctrine* (Salt Lake City: Deseret Book Co., 1963), p. 64.
8. Orson Hyde, in Brigham Young, *Journal of Discourses* (Liverpool, 1854-75), 1:123.
9. Lorenzo Snow, quoted in Anthony A. Hoekema, *The Four Major Cults* (Grand Rapids: Eerdmans, 1963), p. 39.
10. Brigham Young, in *Journal of Discourses,* 1:50.

B. "The Father has a body of flesh and bones as tangible as man's" (D&C 130:22). This is stressed in the Mormon handbook for missionaries as part of the revelation given to Joseph Smith. He saw two personages "of flesh and bones."[11] Thus it is taught that to "deny the materiality of God's person is to deny God; . . . an immaterial body cannot exist" (Talmage 48). (In contrast, note Luke 24: 36-43; John 4:24; 1 Tim. 1:17; 6:16. Also see "D." below—the Holy Spirit.)

C. God is omnipresent. But "this does not mean that the actual person of any one member of the Godhead can be physically present in more than one place at one time" (Talmage 43). Since it is held that "personality" implies "materiality," it must be accepted that "God possesses a form . . . of definite proportions and therefore of limited extension in space" (Talmage 43). His senses and powers, however, are infinite, including that of transferring Himself from place to place. He is likewise omniscient and omnipotent "through the agency of angels and ministering servants," and is thus "in continuous communication with all parts of creation" (Talmage 44).

D. The Holy Spirit is "a personage of Spirit" (D&C 130: 22). He does not have a body of flesh and bones, like the Father and the Son. He is described as "the influence of Deity, the light of Christ, or of Truth, which proceeds forth from the presence of God to fill the immensity of space, and to quicken the understanding of men."[12] Nevertheless, He "can be in only one place at one time" (McConkie 359), although He "emanates from Deity" like "electricity, . . . which fills the earth and the air, and is everywhere present" (McConkie 753).

E. There are many Gods. The following excerpt from McConkie's *Mormon Doctrine* is explicit:

11. *Uniform System for Teaching Investigators* (Salt Lake City: Deseret News Press), p. 31.
12. Smith, *Gospel Doctrine*, p. 60.

> "*Every man who reigns in celestial glory is a god to his
> dominions,*" the Prophet said. (*Teachings,* p. 374.) Hence,
> the Father, who shall continue to all eternity as the God
> of exalted beings, is a *God of Gods.* Further, as the Proph-
> et also taught, there is "*a God above the Father of our
> Lord Jesus Christ. . . .* If Jesus Christ was the Son of God,
> and John discovered that *God the Father of Jesus Christ
> had a Father,* you may suppose that he had a Father also.
> Where was there ever a son without a father? . . . Hence if
> Jesus had a Father, can we not believe that *he* had a
> Father also?" (*Teachings,* pp. 370, 373.) In this way both
> the Father and the Son, as also all exalted beings, are now
> or in due course will become Gods of Gods. (*Teachings,*
> pp. 342-376.) [McConkie 322-23]

Related to this is the declaration that "Abraham and Isaac
and Jacob have entered into their exaltation, and are not
angels, but are gods" (D&C 132:37). In keeping with the
grand scheme of eternal progression, "there never was a
time when there were not Gods and worlds, and when men
were not passing through the same ordeals that we are now
passing through."[13]

F. The Gods have wives! There is a Mother in Heaven!
This is normal teaching related to the fact that God is *literally* the father of our spirits. (See "THE DOCTRINE OF
MAN" below.) "Each god, through his wife or wives,
raises up a numerous family of sons and daughters."[14] "The
begetting of children makes a man a father and a woman
a mother whether we are dealing with man in his mortal or
immortal state" (McConkie 516). God, the exalted and
glorified Man of Holiness, "could not be a Father unless
a Woman of like glory, perfection, and holiness was associated with him as a Mother" (McConkie 516). This "glori-

---

13. Brigham Young, in John A. Widtsoe, ed., *Discourses of Brigham
    Young* (Salt Lake City: Deseret Book Co., 1954), p. 22.
14. Orson Pratt, *The Seer* 1, no. 3 (March 1853):37.

ous truth of celestial parentage" (McConkie 516) is expressed in a Latter-day Saint hymn:

> In the heavens are parents single?
>> No; the thought makes reason stare!
> Truth is reason, truth eternal,
>> Tells me I've a Mother there [In McConkie 517].

Following his statement that Adam is the Mormons' God, Brigham Young declared that Adam "brought Eve, one of his wives, with him."[15] In the same way, mortal beings who gain the ultimate exaltation will become eternal fathers and mothers, and will populate their own worlds with their own spirit children. This involves celestial marriage, the rite by which participants continue on as husband and wife in the celestial kingdom (see "THE DOCTRINE OF THE ATONEMENT" below).

THE DOCTRINE OF JESUS CHRIST

Jesus Christ "is the eternal Jehovah, the promised Messiah, Redeemer and Savior, the Way, the Truth, and the Life" (McConkie 129). Although it may seem to be in keeping with Bible teaching, Mormonism's Christology is nevertheless not that of orthodox Christianity.

A. "Among the spirit children of Elohim, the first-born was and is Jehovah, or Jesus Christ, to whom all others are juniors."[16] This distinction as "first-born" describes Christ's relationship to *all* God's children. Angels and demons, as well as human beings, are included. Various types of beings serve God as angels, or messengers. *All* were the children of the Father. "The devil . . . is a spirit son of God who was born in the morning of pre-existence" (McConkie 192). Devils, or demons, "are the spirit beings who followed Lucifer in his war of rebellion in preexistence" (McConkie 195). One-third of the spirit children of God fol-

15. Brigham Young, in *Journal of Discourses,* 1:50.
16. Smith, *Gospel Doctrine,* p. 70.

lowed Lucifer in that rebellion. The difference between Christ and man or demon is therefore one of degree, or of position, and not of kind. This rejects any thought of His distinctive deity.

B. "By obedience and devotion to the truth he attained that pinnacle of intelligence which ranked him as a God . . . while yet in his pre-existent state" (McConkie 129). It should be noted that this is not the normal pattern. Birth in a mortal body is deemed necessary for the ultimate attainment of godhood. See "THE DOCTRINE OF GOD," sec. A.)

C. Jesus Christ was the executive of the Father in the work of creation. In this work He was aided by Michael (or Adam), "Enoch, Noah, Abraham, Moses, Peter, James, and John, Joseph Smith and many others" (McConkie 169).

D. He was born of the virgin Mary. This assures His *unique* status. It is emphasized, however, that although the conception took place by the power of the Holy Ghost, Christ is not the Son of the Holy Ghost, but of the Father. Talmage adds: "Elohim is LITERALLY the Father of the Spirit of Jesus Christ, and also of the body" (Talmage 466). "He was not born without the aid of a man, and that man was God."[17] Brigham Young adds: "Who is the Father? He is the first of the human family; . . . the same character that was in the garden of Eden, and who is our Father in Heaven."[18]

E. He was altogether sinless. "He is essentially greater than any and all others, by reason (1) of His seniority as the oldest or firstborn; (2) of His unique status in the flesh as the offspring of a mortal mother and of an immortal, or resurrected and glorified, Father; (3) of His selection and foreordination as the one and only Redeemer and

17. Joseph F. Smith, *Doctrines of Salvation* (Salt Lake City: Bookcraft, 1956), 1:18.
18. Brigham Young, in *Journal of Discourses*, 1:50-51.

Savior of the race; and (4) of His transcendent sinlessness" (Talmage 472).

F. He died on the cross, voluntarily and willingly giving His life for the redemption of mankind. (See "THE DOCTRINE OF THE ATONEMENT.")

G. He rose again the third day, with a tangible body of flesh and bones. In addition to the resurrection appearances as recorded in the Bible, the Book of Mormon tells of His coming to the Americas as a resurrected being. He organized the church among the Nephite people, with twelve disciples to lead it (BM 3 Nephi 11).

H. He is coming again in power and great glory to set up His kingdom on earth (see "THE DOCTRINE OF LAST THINGS [ESCHATOLOGY]").

THE DOCTRINE OF MAN

Life began for man and for all created things (animals, fowls, fishes, and every living creature—even the earth itself) at the time of their respective spirit creations. However, it must be understood that God did not create anything, in the sense of bringing into primal existence. He "organized" the elements which are "co-eternal with Him" (McConkie 751). The elements thus "organized" are known as "intelligences," or "spirit children" (McConkie 751).

Note: In the broad sweep of eternity, man's advance in the scheme of eternal progression involves at least four stages: (1) the premortal or spirit existence, with bodies "made of a more pure and refined substance than the elements from which mortal bodies are made. (Ether 3:16; D&C 131:7-8.)" (McConkie 589). (2) Mortal life on earth, with body and spirit temporarily joined together (D&C 93:33). (3) In the spirit world, the abiding place of disembodied spirits, after death. It is "upon this earth," and will be "without inhabitants" after the resurrection (McConkie

762). (4) Immortality, the resurrected state with body and spirit *inseparably* connected.

A. The spirit children of God were given the right of free agency—that is, the freedom to choose good or evil. Their choices determined to a degree their later state. One-third rebelled along with Satan, and fell with him. They will remain "unembodied," never to enter the scheme of eternal progression (see "THE DOCTRINE OF ETERNITY [THE FINAL STATE]," sec. D). Two-thirds stood "affirmatively for Christ," but some were less "valiant" than others. This explains the "millions of insane and afflicted people upon the earth," and "those living in squalor, filth, poverty, and degradation."[19] What they are is the result of choices made in premortal existence. For the same reason, Blacks who are of the lineage of Cain, have been, until 1978, denied the priesthood and its attendant blessings in this mortal state (see addendum, "THE MORMON BLACK AND THE PRIESTHOOD").

B. In the premortal state, Adam was Michael, the archangel (D&C 27:11; 107:54). As the first man, he was formed "in the image of his spiritual Father, God" (Talmage 63). He was placed with one of his preincarnate wives, Eve, in the Garden of Eden. This place, also called Adam-ondi-Ahman, is located in "an area for which Jackson County, Missouri, is the center" (McConkie 20). Zion, the New Jerusalem, will be built there in the latter days.

C. "Adam fell that men might be; and men are, that they might have joy" (BM 2 Nephi 2:25). Adam and Eve had immortal bodies. Eve, however, sinned and became mortal. That created a dilemma for Adam. He had been given two commands: first, multiply and replenish the earth; second, do not touch the forbidden tree. Eve was now mortal. Adam, being yet immortal, could not obey

19. John J. Stewart, *Mormonism and the Negro* (Orem, Utah: Bookmark, 1967), pp. 29-30.

the first command without disobeying the second! "He deliberately and wisely chose to stand by the first and greater commandment, and . . . partook of the fruit" (Talmage 65).

The Fall was foreordained within the purpose of God. It is to be regarded as a good thing in that it was a means of providing billions of preexistent spirits with mortal tabernacles. Adam cried, "Blessed be the name of God, for because of my transgression my eyes are opened, and in this life I shall have joy" (P Moses 5:10). Eve exults, "Were it not for our transgression we never should have had seed, and never should have known good and evil, and the joy of our redemption, and the eternal life which God giveth unto all the obedient" (P Moses 5:11). The Mormon catechism declares that the Fall should be thought of as one of the great advancements toward eternal exaltation and happiness. Man thus became mortal, a blessing in disguise in that it provided the opportunity for eternal progression and perfection to all spirit children of Elohim. It also brought to man the knowledge of good and evil. This "is an essential element in the commission of sin, and our first parents did not have this knowledge until after they had partaken of the fruit" (McConkie 804).

D. The doctrine of original sin is denied by the second article of faith: "We believe that men will be punished for their own sins, and not for Adam's transgression" (P Articles of Faith 2). "Every spirit of man was innocent in the beginning" (D&C 93:38). The age of accountability is reckoned to be eight, since it is stated that "their children shall be baptized for the remission of their sins when eight years old" (D&C 68:27).

THE DOCTRINE OF THE ATONEMENT

We believe that through the Atonement of Christ, all

mankind may be saved, by obedience to the laws and ordinances of the gospel.

We believe that the first principles and ordinances of the gospel are: first, Faith in the Lord Jesus Christ; second, Repentance; third, Baptism by immersion for the remission of sins; fourth, Laying on of hands for the gift of the Holy Ghost [P Articles of Faith 3-4].

In contrast to Lucifer's plan, which would have compelled men to obey God, Christ offered Himself so that men might be free to choose for themselves. There are two aspects of salvation: general, or unconditional; and individual, or conditional.

A. General, or unconditional, salvation is assured for all. Bodily weakness, disease, and physical death came upon all men because of the transgression of Adam. Men become *mortal* (which means that they become subject to "separation of the eternal spirit from the mortal body" (McConkie 185). Christ, by the work of redemption, overcame physical death and *guaranteed* physical resurrection to all living things. This *is* immortality! "Even the unbeliever, the heathen, and the child who dies before reaching the years of discretion, all are redeemed by the Saviour's self-sacrifice from the individual consequences of the Fall. . . . The resurrection of the body is one of the victories achieved by Christ through His atoning sacrifice" (Talmage 85). Included also are "beasts, the fowls of the air, and the fishes of the sea" (D&C 29:23-25), and "the earth . . . and the infinite expanse of the worlds in immensity" (McConkie 642). The only exceptions are the sons of perdition.

B. Individual, or conditional, salvation pertains to the eternal progression of the individual soul and is entirely contingent upon obedience, works, and choices in *this* sphere of existence. The guarantee of immortality (physical resurrection) is not synonymous with "eternal life," or "exaltation." It does not assure "godhood" in eternity.

There are three possible spheres of existence in eternity. Only one, the celestial, is the abode of those who continue in the eternal progression to be as "gods." (See "THE DOC-TRINE OF ETERNITY [THE FINAL STATE]" below.) Entrance to this sphere is on the basis of obedience to the laws and ordinances, and "by devotion and faithfulness, by endur-ing to the end in righteousness and obedience, it is then possible to merit a celestial reward" (McConkie 116; see also D&C 20:29; BM 2 Nephi 9:23-24). It is with this in mind that Talmage asserts that "the sectarian dogma of justification by faith alone has exercised an influence for evil" (Talmage 479). Where one goes after he is resur-rected is determined by his individual responses, actions, and choices *now*.

C. "To the Mormons, baptism . . . is the most vital and significant of all ordinances—the very gateway into the kingdom of heaven—an indispensable step in our salva-tion and exaltation."[20] Without it, forgiveness of sins is impossible. As Joseph Smith stated, "They who believe not on your words, and are not baptized in water in my [Jesus'] name, for the remission of their sins, that they may receive the Holy Ghost, shall be damned" (D&C 84:74). Infant baptism is considered a "gross perversion" of true Christian doctrine.

Baptism for the dead is the "welding link" between "fathers and children" (D&C 128:18). This unique prac-tice occupies a prominent place in current Mormon temple activity, and presumably will be the great work during the Millennium. The basic teaching is that many have died without the opportunity to hear and believe the gospel. To them, in the spirit-world, Christ went and preached

20. Wallace F. Bennett, *Why I Am a Mormon* (Boston: Beacon Press, 1958), p. 124.

after His death. First Corinthians 15:29 and 1 Peter 3:18-22 are claimed as supporting this. There are others "who have gone into the spirit world who have never submitted to the ordinance of baptism, while vast numbers of those who have been baptized had the ordinance administered by one who held no rightful authority whatever."[21] They also are given opportunity to hear and to believe. But even spirit believers cannot be saved without water baptism. Therefore baptism by proxy is a major activity for which

> the Latter-day Saints are assiduously engaged in erecting temples wherein this ordinance may be performed. . . . The Saints are flocking to the temples of the Lord and redeeming their dead from the grasp of Satan. They are performing a great and mighty work for the human family who have lived upon the earth in the different ages of the world's history, and who, in some instances, by revelation, make manifest to their children or friends the fact that they have accepted the Gospel in the spirit world.[22]

In pursuit of this activity, the "Church has accumulated more than 150,000 rolls of microfilm covering more than 230 million pages of vital statistics, and the work is still going on."[23] There were said to have been 3,607,962 such baptisms during 1965.

D. "Celestial marriage is the gate to an exaltation in the highest heaven within the celestial world" (McConkie 118; see also D&C 131:1-4). This rite is performed only in Mormon temples. By it the man and woman are "sealed for time and eternity" and "have eternal claim on their posterity, and the gift of eternal increase."[24] Provided they keep all the other terms and conditions set forth, they be-

---

21. John Morgan, *The Plan of Salvation* (Salt Lake City: Deseret News Press, n.d.), p. 22.
22. Ibid., p. 23.
23. Bennett, p. 130.
24. Smith, *Doctrines of Salvation*, 2:44.

come "gods in their own right" (McConkie 118). This exalting ordinance can also be performed vicariously, for the benefit of worthy dead.

THE DOCTRINE OF LAST THINGS (ESCHATOLOGY)

We believe in the literal gathering of Israel and in the restoration of the Ten Tribes; that Zion will be built upon this [the American] continent; that Christ will reign personally upon the earth; and that the earth will be renewed and receive its paradisiacal glory [P Articles of Faith 10].

A. The gatherings are three in number: "the house of Joseph will be established in America, the house of Judah in Palestine, and . . . the Lost Tribes will come to Ephraim in America to receive their blessings in due course" (McConkie 306; from D&C 133).

1. The people of Israel will assemble in the land of Zion, which is the North American continent. It is pointed out that upon Ephraim, the son of Joseph, was conferred the birthright in Israel (Gen. 48:5-22). The Northern Kingdom of Israel, later scattered over all the known world, was frequently referred to as Ephraim. Thus Ephraim "stands at head in the Latter days . . . and must be gathered first to prepare the way . . . for the rest of the tribes of Israel."[25] Further, "Joseph Smith was pure Ephraimite,"[26] of the lineage of Joseph, and "the great majority of those who have come into the Church are Ephraimites."[27] Thus the House of Israel is being gathered as men and women join The Church of Jesus Christ of Latter-day Saints, and the house of Israel is being established in Zion.

2. The house of Judah (the Jewish people) are now being gathered to Jerusalsm, mostly in unbelief. "The great body of [them] will not receive Christ as their Redeemer

---

25. Smith, *Doctrines of Salvation*, 3:252.
26. Ibid., p. 253.
27. Ibid., p. 252.

until he comes himself and makes himself manifest unto them."[28]

3. The lost ten tribes are descendants of people carried away captive by Shalmaneser of Assyria (721 B.C.). Many are still living in "the north countries," where the Lord has hidden them. Proof of their existence is found in the Book of Mormon (BM 3 Nephi 16:1-4; 17:4). They were visited by the resurrected Lord after his ministry on this continent among the Nephites. "In due course [they] will return and come to the children of Ephraim to receive their blessings. This great gathering will take place under the direction of the President of The Church of Jesus Christ of Latter-day Saints" (McConkie 458).

B. The millennial reign of Christ will follow the gathering of Israel and establishment of an earthly Zion.

1. The first resurrection will inaugurate this glorious period of peace and prosperity. Called the "resurrection of life," or "of the just," it will be in two parts. Those being resurrected with celestial bodies will come forth in the morning of the first resurrection. They will be caught up to meet the Lord, and will descend with Him, to reign together with Him (D&C 88:95-98). Apparently included are all children who die before reaching the age of accountability. In the afternoon, those with "terrestrial bodies" will rise (see "THE DOCTRINE OF ETERNITY [THE FINAL STATE]," sec. B). They live on the earth during the millennial reign.

2. The second coming of Christ will be marked by destruction of the wicked. This event will occur at the end of the Battle of Armageddon, which will then be in progress. The earth will be cleansed of all its corruption and wickedness. All the wicked, not worthy of either celestial or terrestrial glory, will spend the thousand years in "the prison house prepared for them." There they are to "re-

28. Ibid., p. 9.

pent and cleanse themselves through the things which they shall suffer."[29]

3. The earth will be cleansed by fire, renewed, and given its paradisiacal glory, a return to the "edenic, terrestrial state."

4. Satan will be bound, his powers limited for the 1,000 years. Men will be to a degree relieved from temptation, but "sin will not be wholly abolished, nor will death be banished" (Talmage 371). "Children will live to reach maturity in the flesh, and then may be changed to a condition of immortality" (Talmage 371).

5. "Mortal and immortal beings will tenant the earth, and communion with heavenly powers will be common" (Talmage 371).

6. The great work of the Millennium will be the vicarious performing of "saving and exalting ordinances" (baptism and celestial marriage) on behalf of "worthy dead who did not have opportunity during life" (McConkie 501).

7. The gospel will be taught with great power, and "eventually all people will embrace the truth."[30]

8. The second resurrection takes place at the end of the Millennium. As in the case of the first resurrection, it has two parts. Those who are destined for telestial glory (see "THE DOCTRINE OF ETERNITY [THE FINAL STATE]," sec. C are raised in the "fore part." In the "latter end" comes the resurrection of damnation, pertaining to the sons of perdition.

9. Satan will be released, and will lead the final rebellion at the end of the Millennium. He will deceive men again and will gather together "his armies, even the hosts of hell" (McConkie 501). His defeat will be total. All, including Satan, will be cast into "punishment so terrible

29. Ibid., p. 60.
30. Ibid., p. 64.

that the knowledge is withheld from all except those who are consigned to this doom" (Talmage 60).

C. The earth will die, be resurrected, and become "a celestialized body fit for the abode of the most exalted intelligences" (Talmage 375). "The Millennium, with all its splendor, is but a more advanced stage of preparation, by which the earth and its inhabitants will approach foreordained perfection" (Talmage 375).

THE DOCTRINE OF ETERNITY (THE FINAL STATE)

There are three eternal kingdoms of widely differing glories, and another place for the sons of perdition. The status and place of the individual in eternity is the outcome of his own efforts, and "not Christ's sacrifice."[31] Each kingdom is organized on a plan of gradation. Advancement within each is possible, but progress from one to another lacks "positive affirmation" (Talmage 409).

A. The celestial kingdom (the sphere of exaltation) will be located on the "resurrected" earth. It will be the abode of those who have been cleansed of sins and have continued obedient to the laws and ordinances of the gospel. "They shall be gods, because they have no end" (D&C 132: 16-26). "They have eternal increase . . . ; that is, they have spirit children in the resurrection, in relation to which offspring they stand in the same position that God our Father stands to us" (McConkie 257). All who attain unto this sphere shall dwell in the presence of God and His Christ forever (D&C 76:62).

B. The terrestrial kingdom will be peopled by those who did not accept the gospel until they were in the spirit world. With them will be "accountable persons who die without law; . . . . honorable men of the earth who are blinded . . . and who therefore do not accept and live the gospel law" (McConkie 784); and members of The Church

31. Bennett, p. 191.

of Jesus Christ of Latter-day Saints who were not valiant,
but were lukewarm. They remain unmarried and without
exaltation; and they receive the presence of the Son, but
not the fullness of the Father.

C. The telestial kingdom is the place to which "most
of the adult people who have lived from the day of Adam
. . . will go" (McConkie 778). Joseph Smith saw in a
vision that the inhabitants of the telestial world "were as
innumerable as the stars in the firmament of heaven, or as
the sand upon the seashore" (D&C 76:109). Having rejected Christ and lived wickedly, they will be the last to
be resurrected, and they will have suffered the wrath of
God in the spirit world. In this sphere they will never
know the presence of God or of Christ, but shall continue
as servants of God.

D. *Perdition* signifies that there is no hope of any degree
of salvation. "Two persons, Cain and Satan, have received
the title *Perdition*" (McConkie 566). The sons of perdition include the angels who rebelled with Satan, and men
who commit unpardonable sin—that is, "having received
the testimony of Christ, and having been endowed by the
Holy Spirit, [they] then deny the same and defy the power
of God" (Talmage 410). The unpardonable sin "can be
committed by those only who have received knowledge
and conviction of the truth" (Talmage 410). They are
doomed to everlasting fire.

However, this is softened by the idea that "there must be
an end to future punishment." It is called "eternal punishment" because God is "eternal." "Eternal punishment" is
simply "God's punishment; . . . it is the name of the punishment God inflicts, he being eternal in his nature." God
has the power to pardon beyond the grave! Eternal punishment may endure "one hour, one day, one week, one
year, or an age."[32]

32. Morgan, pp. 23-24.

POLYGAMY

The practice of polygamy, or plural marriage, "was established as a result of direct revelation, and many of those who followed the same felt they were divinely commanded to do so" (Talmage 424). The record is found in the *Doctrine and Covenants*, section 132. Its heading reads: "Revelation given through Joseph Smith the Prophet at Nauvoo, Illinois, recorded July 12, 1843, relating to the new and everlasting covenant, including the eternity of the marriage covenant, as also plurality of wives." In this revelation it is clear that one of the "essentials for the attainment of the status of godhood" is "marriage duly authorized" (D&C 132). In verses 52 to 54 of section 132, Emma Smith, Joseph's wife, is told that she must prepare to receive additional wives "given" to her husband, otherwise she would be destroyed.

It has been noted that the gods of Mormonism are polygamous, and are constantly begetting children. The second president, Brigham Young, is credited with the statement that "when our father Adam came into the Garden of Eden, ... he brought Eve, *one of his wives*, with him."[33] Thus it is that the concept that Jesus Christ was married and that he was a polygamist, evokes no consternation. Only by begetting children could he attain unto the utmost in the celestial kingdom.

Polygamy became a controversial issue in later Mormon history. But there is no doubt that the practice was common and that it began with Joseph Smith the Prophet. The sixth president of the church, Joseph F. Smith, wrote: "I can positively state, on indisputable evidence, that Joseph Smith was the author, under God, of the revelation on plural marriage."[34] He cites an affidavit concerning one plural wife of Joseph Smith. He also gives the names of

33. Brigham Young, in *Journal of Discourses*, 1:50.
34. Smith, *Gospel Doctrine*, p. 489.

six other women who testified, under oath, "that they were sealed during his lifetime to the Prophet Joseph Smith."[35] Polygamy continued as a church observance in Utah for ten years without any law being enacted in opposition to it. Beginning with 1862, however, federal statutes were framed declaring the practice unlawful. After many appeals by the church had been unsuccessful, Mormon president Wilford Woodruff, the only man on earth holding the keys of sealing ordinances, issued an official declaration in 1890. Thereupon the church discontinued the practice of plural marriage, according to James E. Talmage, one of the twelve apostles of the Mormon Church (Talmage 424, 524-25).

The Mormon Black and the Priesthood

As noted above, Joseph Smith was ordained to the Aaronic priesthood by John the Baptist and to the Melchizedek priesthood by Peter, James, and John. Those two priesthoods are central in the organization of the Mormons. "As pertaining to eternity, the priesthood is the eternal power and authority of Deity by which all things exist; by which they are created, governed, and controlled; by which the universe and worlds without number have come rolling into existence; by which the great plan of creation, redemption, and exaltation operates throughout immensity. It is the power of God" (McConkie 594).

The lesser priesthood is the Aaronic, containing the offices of deacon, teacher, priest, and bishop. It is preparatory—by it one is trained for the greater, the Melchizedek priesthood. This latter has within it the offices of elder, seventy, high priest, patriarch or evangelist, and apostle. The Melchizedek priesthood is "the channel through which all knowledge, doctrine, the plan of salvation, and every

35. Ibid., pp. 489-90.

important matter is revealed from heaven" (McConkie 476). Mormon Doctrine specifically declares "that those spirits sent to earth through the lineage of Cain and of Ham are absolutely denied the priesthood as far as mortal life is concerned" (McConkie 479). The Mormon Church further holds that there were premortal spirits who were "less valiant" than others, and who "thereby had certain spiritual restrictions imposed upon them during mortality." They "are known to us as the *negroes*" (McConkie 527). Blacks are denied the priesthood, and "under no circumstances can they hold this delegation of authority" (McConkie 527). They are "not equal with other races where the receipt of certain spiritual blessings are concerned" (McConkie 527). This is the Lord's doing, and is based on His eternal laws of justice!

It is all the more remarkable that on June 9, 1978, Mormon president Spencer W. Kimball, Prophet, Seer, and Revelator of the Church of Jesus Christ of Latter-day Saints, issued this decree: God "by revelation has confirmed that the long-promised day has come when every faithful, worthy man may receive the holy priesthood, with power to exercise its divine authority. . . . Accordingly, all worthy members of the Church may be ordained to the priesthood without regard for race or color."[36] This long-expected decree was widely promulgated, and was hailed by the fewer than one thousand black members of the church. Apparently no attempt has been made to reconcile these diametrically opposed edicts of "the will and word of the Lord" and His eternal laws of justice. Inasmuch as mortal existence was defined by irreversible actions made in the preexistent spirit world, no doubt explanations are impossible.

36. *Forward Magazine* 2, no. 1 (1978), p. 1. The magazine is published by Christian Research Institute, Box 500, San Juan Capistrano, Calif. 92675.

DIVISIONS IN MORMONISM

At the death of Joseph Smith, a special conference voted on August 8, 1844, at Nauvoo, Illinois, to accept the church council of twelve apostles, headed by Brigham Young, as the interim governing body pending reorganization of a presidency. The main body, numbering some twenty thousand, went with Young to Utah. These composed the beginning of the group usually alluded to when mention is made of "the Mormons." Membership today is approximately two million.

Five dissenting groups refused to follow Brigham Young and formed separate organizations. Of these, only one is significant. It is The Reorganized Church of Jesus Christ of Latter Day Saints, with headquarters at Independence, Missouri. They are called Josephites. The original thousand followed Emma Smith, Joseph's first wife, and were later organized by Joseph Smith, Jr. Today the membership is approximately 175,000. An active publication program emphasizes the differences that exist between themselves and the Utah Mormon Church, as the main body is designated.

Both groups believe in the authenticity of the Book of Mormon. Both accept and publish "many of the revelations given through the Prophet Joseph Smith in our respective versions and additions of the *Doctrine and Covenants*."[37] Differences relate to conflicting views concerning God, the question of polygamy, secret temple rites, and prophetic succession and leadership. Strong exception is taken to the "axiom current among Mormons for many years, 'As man is, God once was; as God is, man may become.' "[38] The teaching that God is Himself a progressive being is rejected. The Reorganized Church teaches that

37. Elbert A. Smith, *Differences That Persist* (Independence, Mo.: Herald Publishing House), p. 6.
38. Ibid., p. 9.

God is eternally unchangeable. With this naturally goes the repudiation of Brigham Young's Adam-God theology. Correlated with this is the denial of the doctrine of celestial marriage as related to the eternal progression and exaltation of men.

The Reorganized Church maintains that polygamy is contrary to the teaching and practice of Joseph Smith. Documental evidence is offered to prove that the accepted story of the plural wives of the Prophet was a deception perpetrated by Brigham Young and his immediate associates. Section 132 of the *Doctrine and Covenants* is not accepted as divine revelation.

In the Kirtland Temple of the Reorganized Church there are no secret meetings of any kind. All meetings are open to the public; none of the sacraments and ordinances is conducted in secret. The "Secret Temple Rites" as practiced by the Mormons of Utah are held to be abhorrent. Finally, the Josephites disavow the claim that Young and his successors are the ordained elders of the church. They followed Joseph Smith, Jr., as the designated successor of his father, and have maintained their own line of "revealed" succession.

This group publishes and uses the Inspired Version of the Bible. Started by Joseph Smith as a revision of the King James Version, it was not completed by him and is therefore not used by the Utah Mormons.

2

Jehovah's Witnesses

JEHOVAH'S WITNESSES are, by their own definition, "servants of Jehovah, the Almighty God, and active witnesses to his sovereign supremacy."[1] Claiming to be followers of "Christ their Leader," they reject any association with the "religious hypocrites of organized Christendom." Anti-Christ is defined as "any organization or individual that is against Christ or Christianity." This includes those who say that "Christ was God incarnate; deny Christ actually came to earth as a Perfect Man of Flesh; the Collective Clergy of Christendom; Pagan Religions; Communistic Red Religion"; and supporters of the United Nations (MS 14-15).

God's sovereignty, they say, was impugned when Adam and Eve rebelled. Therefore the major issue before all heaven and earth is the vindication of the name and sovereignty of Jehovah. *This* is more important than the salvation of men, and will be completely settled at the coming Battle of Armageddon. In the meantime, the faithful members of this organization are demonstrating that there is "a group of persons dedicated to do God's will"[2] and thus are vindicating "his reproached and misrepresented name" (LG 29).

The publication activity of the Jehovah's Witnesses is

1. *Make Sure of All Things* (Brooklyn: Watchtower Bible and Tract Society, 1953), p. 193 (hereafter cited as MS).
2. *Let God Be True* (Brooklyn: Watchtower Bible and Tract Society, 1952), p. 219 (hereafter cited as LG).

simply amazing. The average printing of each issue of *Awake* magazine is 10,125,000 (1977), and the average printing of each issue of *The Watchtower* magazine is 9,200,000 (1978) in 82 languages. The production of cloth-bound books is apparently endless, with considerable repetition of contents. All are written in the same authoritative tone, very convincing to uninformed readers. In vehement and caustic language, particular exception is taken to the orthodox doctrine of the Trinity. The essential deity of Jesus Christ is denied, as is the personality of the Holy Spirit. The efficacy of the atonement is vitiated by the demand for continued faithfulness in witnessing, and any degree of assurance of salvation is virtually impossible. There is unscriptural stress on the 144,000 "followers of Christ" who "only will go to heaven" (MS 196). *They* compose the "body of Christ," and for them are reserved the titles which, in orthodox Christianity, are applied to all true believers. The mass of the Jehovah's Witnesses work incessantly, with the hope of eternity on an earthly paradise. And continuance even there seems contingent upon faithfulness.[3] This "faithfulness in witnessing" is indicated in the reported 307,272,262 hours of witnessing during 1978.

The organization known as Jehovah's Witnesses was legally incorporated in 1884 by Charles Taze Russell. It was then known as The Watch Tower Bible and Tract Society. Russell rejected much of the teaching of orthodox Christianity and built his own system of Bible interpretation. His ideas were widely circulated through a seven-volume *Studies in the Scriptures* (Allegheny, Pa.: Watchtower Bible and Tract Society). "It is said that 15 million copies of this series have been distributed."[4] The organiza-

3. *From Paradise Lost to Paradise Regained* (Brooklyn: Watchtower Bible and Tract Society, 1958), p. 226.
4. Bruce M. Metzger, *The Jehovah's Witnesses and Jesus Christ* (Princeton, N.J.: Theological Book Agency), p. 65. The booklet is a reprint from *Theology Today* 10, no. 1 (April 1953):65-85.

tion was variously known as Russellites, Millennial Dawnists, Rutherfordites (after Joseph Franklin Rutherford, the successor to Russell), and International Bible Students. However, in 1931 the official name became Jehovah's Witnesses. This was based on Isaiah 43:10 (see also 44:8) which reads: "Ye are my witnesses, saith the LORD [Jehovah]." Rutherford, president since 1917, was succeeded by Nathan Homer Knorr in 1942. Under his presidency the work expanded into at least "lands and islands of the sea." Knorr died in June 1977. He has been succeeded by Frederick Franz, a Jehovah's Witness since 1913.

SOURCES OF AUTHORITY

"Let God have the say as to what is the truth that sets men free" (LG 9). "Accept His Word, the Bible, as the truth" (LG 9). By these and by similar statements the Jehovah's Witnesses purport to reveal their devotion to the Bible. It is "Jehovah's God's written word to mankind, revealing himself and expressing his purpose" (MS 36).

Actually, the ultimate source of authority is the Word of God as translated and interpreted in voluminous writings of the organization. As stated by Pastor Russell concerning his *Studies in the Scriptures,* "People cannot see the divine plan by studying the Bible itself."[5] The *Studies* contain this declaration: "Be it known that no other system of theology even claims, or has ever attempted to harmonize in itself *every* statement of the Bible, yet nothing short of this can we claim."[6] The *New World Translation of the Holy Scriptures* was published by the Watchtower Bible and Tract Society in 1961. The title page states that the translation is "rendered from the Original Languages by the New World Bible Translation Committee." It is a

5. *Watchtower,* September 15, 1910. Quoted by J. Oswald Sanders, *Cults and Isms* (Grand Rapids: Zondervan, 1962), p. 79.
6. Charles Taze Russell, *Studies in the Scriptures* (Allegheny, Pa. Watchtower Bible and Tract Society, 1907), 1:348.

biased translation, made to verify predetermined doctrines. As Dr. Anthony A. Hoekema writes, "Many of the peculiar teachings of the Watchtower Society are smuggled into the text of the Bible itself."[7] Unwarranted liberties are taken in the English translation to substantiate teaching which is not in keeping with that of historic Christianity but is dogmatically stated in Jehovah's-Witness writings.

For instance, the book *Make Sure of All Things* categorically declares that "the Holy Spirit is NOT a person" (MS 389). Therefore the word *spirit*, indicating the Holy Spirit, is *never* capitalized. Again, since the deity of Jesus Christ is denied, John 1:1 is translated, "In the beginning the Word was . . . and the Word was a god." It has been pointed out that in Colossians 1:15-17 the word "other" has been inserted, without warrant, four times. This is done in order to put Jesus Christ on a level with "other" created things. Philippians 2:6 is another flagrantly false translation. It reads: "[Christ Jesus] although he was existing in God's form, gave no consideration to a seizure, namely, that he should be equal to God." The obvious meaning is that Christ was not equal with God, and did not choose to be.

These examples are given to indicate that the source of authority for Jehovah's Witnesses is not the Bible, but the Bible as interpreted by Russell, Rutherford, and their followers. Russell's "sanctified common sense" rejected the mystery of the Trinity, and with it he eliminated the very person of the Holy Spirit, who convicts of sin (John 16:8), and denigrated the deity of the Son, without which there can be no atonement. (Further information relative to Jehovah's-Witness teaching about the Holy Spirit and the Son is given below, under "THE DOCTRINE OF GOD" and "THE DOCTRINE OF JESUS CHRIST.")

7. Anthony A. Hoekema, *The Four Major Cults* (Grand Rapids: Eerdmans, 1963), pp. 238-39.

THE DOCTRINE OF GOD

The name *Jehovah* means "the Purposer." He is the only true God, "and is now working out his purpose of vindicating his name and sovereignty and blessing all faithful mankind through his kingdom" (MS 193). He is *not* a triune god, which "false doctrine would deny his almighty supremacy" (MS 188). The doctrine of the Trinity originated in "ancient Babylonish paganism" (MS 386).

A. Who is Jehovah? This question, asked by Pharaoh of Egypt, epitomizes the attitude of the world today. It began with the rebellion in Eden, which "called into question Jehovah's position as supreme sovereign."[8] Could Jehovah create a people who would serve Him faithfully in total obedience? This was the primary issue even before creation. That the answer is positive is being demonstrated by His "witnesses" as they are declaring His name throughout the earth.

B. Jehovah is *one* person. His principal attributes are love, wisdom, justice, and power. At one time all alone in the universal space, He was self-contained and never lonely.[9] He is above all; He is supreme sovereign of the universe. He is omniscient, but *not* omnipresent, although His power extends everywhere (MS 191). The doctrine of the Trinity is brushed aside as being "false, unbiblical." Proof of this involves, for the most part, denial of the equality of the Son and the Father. The doctrinal handbook *Make Sure of All Things* (1953 edition, revised in 1957) succinctly states, "Jesus Inferior to Jehovah," "Jehovah is Christ's God" (MS 387-88). Added to this is the consistent denial of the personality of the Holy Spirit.

C. The Holy Spirit is *not* a person; rather, He is subject to God (MS 387-88). The Spirit is defined as "Jehovah's in-

8. Virgilius Ferm, ed., *Religion in the Twentieth Century* (New York: Philosophical Library, 1948), p. 388.
9. *New Heavens and a New Earth* (Brooklyn: Watchtower Bible and Tract Society, 1953), p. 21 (hereafter cited as NH).

visible energizing force ... that produces visible results ... experienced by men" (MS 360). Thus in the New World Translation of the Holy Scriptures Genesis 1:2 reads, in part, "and God's active force was moving to and fro over the surface of the waters." As indicated above, in the *New World Translation* references to the Holy Spirit are never capitalized. There is no attempt to explain the Spirit's activities as helper, guide, advocate, and comforter, nor is it shown how He convicts of sin, speaks to and through believers, may be grieved, and so forth. (See John 14:16-17, 26; 16:7-15; Acts 13:2; Eph. 4:30; and many other verses.)

THE DOCTRINE OF CREATION

Jehovah God created all that exists. He, the great First Cause, brought into existence all that is material and spiritual in the universe. In the divine order, there were three stages in creation:

A. The only-begotten Son was the first creation. Jesus Christ is God's first creation. Having received life directly from God "unassisted," he was given "priority and pre-eminence among all God's creatures."[10] By this creation, Jehovah God became a father. Being endowed with wisdom, the Son became the master workman, the co-worker with Jehovah through whom all else came into existence.

B. Angels, of different ranks, were created next. Shortly after the "dawn of creation," Lucifer, son of the morning, was brought into being. He and the only-begotten Son were the princes, and were called "morning stars," who worked together and "sang together."[11] (See Job 38:7.) Then all other spirit sons of God, seraphim, cherubim, and angels (messengers), were brought forth "perfect, glorious, and holy."[12] They are numbered in the hundreds of mil-

---

10. *The New World* (Brooklyn: Watchtower Bible and Tract Society, 1942), p. 16.
11. Ibid., p. 18.
12. Ibid., p. 24.

lions, all organized and placed in positions of service.

C. Finally, the heavens and earth were created. At God's command, his "mighty Son, the Word," began to adorn the fathomless depths of space with the material creation."[13] Billions of milky ways and galaxies of stars! It should be noted that any suggestion of evolution is untenable. However, the "silence" of Genesis 1:1 "may allow" for the estimate of "modern science" that the average age of the Milky Way is 3 to 4 billion years (NH 34-35).

Of interest is the calculation that each of the Creator's workdays was 7,000 years long. Reckoning that God's "sabbath rest" began some 6,000 years ago, the Battle of Armageddon is near "and Christ's reign of 1,000 years will begin immediately after it." The Sabbath rest is therefore 7,000 years long. On this basis, man was "put on the earth toward the end of 42,000 years of earth's preparation" (LG 168).

THE DOCTRINE OF JESUS CHRIST

"Jesus, the Christ, a created individual, is the second greatest Personage of the universe. Jehovah God and Jesus together constitute the Superior Authorities" (MS 207).

The consistent and vehement denial of the deity of Christ is an outstanding feature of this system. In that denial, Jehovah's Witnesses have revived the ancient heresy known as Arianism. To the Witnesses, Jesus Christ was a Jew whose life and teachings have affected the course of all human history. He was one who had a wonderful past before he appeared on earth. But he was not Jehovah God, nor was he equal with Jehovah God. In fact, he was known as Michael, the archangel! (NH 28).

The following headings are taken from pages 207-10 of *Make Sure of All Things* (revised April 1, 1957), which sets

13. *The Truth Shall Make You Free* (Brooklyn: Watchtower Bible and Tract Society, 1943), p. 54.

forth seventy principal themes and gives a "balanced picture" of the belief of Jehovah's Witnesses:

A. *First-born Son of God, a Spirit.* Jesus Christ was a spirit person, the most beloved and most favored of all creation. He was the Word, or the Logos. "As such, he was a god, but not the Almighty God, who is Jehovah" (LG 33). Note likewise that he did not possess immortality (deathlessness).

B. *Lesser than Jehovah.* That Jesus Christ is lesser than Jehovah is substantiated by an unjustifiable translation of Philippians 2:6. "Christ Jesus . . . gave no consideration to a seizure, namely, that he should be equal to God." That is, "he did not follow the course of the Devil and plot and scheme to make himself like or equal to the Most High God" (LG 34-35). Reference is also made to the erroneous, indefensible translation of John 1:1, "In the beginning was the Word . . . and the Word was a god." While seeking to deprive the Word of equality with the Father, it actually makes Jehovah's Witnesses to be polytheistic.[14]

C. *Born as a Human Son of God, Oct., 2 B.C.* "At the time that the young woman conceived by the miracle-working power of Almighty God then the life of the Son of God was transferred from his glorious position with God his Father in heaven to the embryo of a human" (LG 36). To call this an "incarnation of God" is "unscriptural," for "the Son of God laid aside completely his spirit existence."[15] He was born as a mere human creature, the "full equal of the perfect Adam in Eden, sinless and possessed of the right to perfect human life in Paradise."[16] Jesus forfeited that right in order to become the basis of redemption, as will be noted under "THE DOCTRINE OF SALVATION."

D. *Became the Messiah Seed in Fall, A.D. 29.* By his

---

14. See Metzger.
15. *The Truth Shall Make You Free*, pp. 245-46.
16. Ibid., p. 249.

water baptism, Jesus indicated his submission to do God's will. God thereupon consecrated Him by His "holy spirit" and acknowledged Him as His beloved Son. God "begot Jesus to be his spiritual Son once more instead of a human Son" (LG 38). Jesus was anointed to be the long-promised King in God's Kingdom—and to become the Messiah. Henceforth, he was Jesus Christ, or Jesus the Anointed.

E. *Died on Stake as Ransomer in Spring, A.D. 33.* By definition, the cross is a symbol falsely used to represent Christianity. Jesus was not crucified on a cross; rather, He was impaled on a stake. This stake is depicted as a single upright pole, with no crossbar.

When John the Baptist said, "Behold the Lamb of God" (John 1:36), he showed the *secondary* purpose for which the Son of God came to earth—that is, to die for sinful men.

F. *Resurrected Immortal on Third Day.* On the third day, Jesus' immortal Father, Jehovah God, raised Him from the dead, not as a human Son, but as a mighty immortal *spirit* Son. "For forty days thereafter he materialized, as angels before him had done, to show himself alive to his disciples as witnesses" (LG 40). God raised Him to deathless heavenly life as a glorious spirit creature, exalted to be next highest to Himself, the Most High God.

It is to be observed that the materialization of Jesus' body after the resurrection was a temporary thing. What became of his physical body? "We know nothing about what became of it, except that it did not decay or corrupt. . . . Whether it was dissolved into gases or whether it is preserved somewhere as a grand memorial of God's love . . . no one knows."[17]

Since there is no bodily resurrection, there can be no second coming in the scriptural sense of that term.

17. Russell, 2:129.

THE DOCTRINE OF MAN

Toward the end of the sixth creative day, nearly 42,000 years after the beginning of creation, God made man in His own image. Man was given dominion over the earth and its forms of life, with the attributes of wisdom, justice, love, and power. (See above under "THE DOCTRINE OF CREATION.")

A. 1. Man *is* a soul. He consists of a "body together with the life principle or life force activating it" (MS 349). This is a fundamental precept of Jehovah's Witnesses. "Man has no soul within him that is separate and distinct from his human body, and that could exist independently, should the dissolution of the body occur."[18] Death is simply cessation of existence.

2. Man is *not* immortal, any more than are fish, birds, or animals. All are "earthly souls," having organisms of flesh which are "kept living by means of blood circulating in their systems" (MS 349). That is, man does not possess, in any sense, the quality of deathlessness, or incorruptibility. Such a teaching is held to have been originated by Satan in the Garden. Note, above, that even Jesus Christ was not given immortality until the time of the resurrection. Angels also are mortal and destructible.

It should be underlined that orthodox Christianity maintains the doctrine of the inherent immortality of human souls. Genesis 2:7 states that God formed man of the dust of the earth and breathed into his nostrils the breath of life. The body, created from the dust, is mortal and subject to death (separation of soul from body); the soul (the breath of life), is immortal, indestructible, yet subject to spiritual death (separation from God). Man sinned. Lest he eat of the tree of life and thus gain immortality of the body, he was expelled from the Garden of Eden (Gen. 3: 22-23).

18. MS 349; see also *The Truth Shall Make You Free*, p. 75.

3. Immortality is given as a reward for faithfulness to Christ. But it must be noted that *only* the 144,000 can ever receive immortality. Immortality is inseparably linked with the kingdom of heaven, and flesh and blood creatures cannot enter. *Human* souls can only dwell forever on the earth. (See below—the 144,000.)

B. 1. Had Adam not sinned, he would have lived on earth forever in his mortal state. So would all his children.

2. By Adam's disobedience, the sentence of death was passed upon all mankind. Death is called soul-sleep, the "termination of existence, utter cessation of conscious, intellectual or physical activity" of any kind (MS 86). In this connection, note that the resurrection of the body is thus actually re-creation according to the "memory" of God, not restoration of the "original identical body" (MS 311).

Figuring on the basis that one of God's ways of measuring time reckons "one day . . . as a thousand years" (2 Pet. 3:8), it is declared that Adam actually died during the day in which he sinned. He died when he was 930 years old, in the year 309 B.C.E. (Before Our Common Era). He literally ceased to exist, "without hope of resurrection."[19]

3. When Satan induced man to sin, he actually challenged God. Could Jehovah put on earth a man who could not be turned away from Him? God's sovereignty was impugned, and thus the vindication of His name became an issue before the universe.

THE DOCTRINE OF SALVATION

"Salvation is the deliverance from the destructive power of sin, a redemption from the ultimate end of sin which is everlasting death, annihilation" (MS 330).

A. The Ransom paid for all. The Fall brought death

19. *Things in Which It Is Impossible for God to Lie* (Brooklyn: Watchtower Bible and Tract Society), pp. 177-78.

to all men, and the possibility of perfect human life with all its rights and earthly prospects was lost. But on the cross Christ made atonement for sin. That is, He provided a ransom which canceled death and gave to man *the opportunity to receive* the gift of life. It must be noted carefully that the ransom price was "his human life poured out in willing sacrifice" (LG 116). He did not deserve to die. But His perfect human life with all its *earthly* prospects and rights was laid down in death, and "*was not taken back* by Jesus at His resurrection, for he was raised a divine spirit creature."[20] He willingly forfeited His perfect human life on earth and thus offset the inherited condemnation for Adam's family. He exchanged "his human existence for the spirit existence, and by relinquishing His right to live, he secured man an opportunity to live" in the paradise that will be located on the earth.[21] He made it possible for most men to attain salvation.

B. The ransom does not avail for all. Salvation is a goal to be attained by those who faithfully carry out their dedication to do God's will. It is a goal made possible by the atonement of Christ, but it is guaranteed only to the faithful ones who endure to the end. Adam is characteristic of those not included among the ransomed. He deliberately forfeited the perfect life God had given him. Eve did likewise. The people of Noah's day, those who lived in Sodom, the religious hypocrites of Jesus' day, and those who are killed at Armageddon are beyond redemption. They have received, or will receive, a "destruction that lasts forever"[22]—eternal annihilation.

C. Only the 144,000 will share in heavenly glory with Jesus Christ. (All other Jehovah's Witnesses will enjoy the blessings of life on the earth.)

20. John H. Gerstner, *The Theology of the Major Sects* (Grand Rapids: Baker, 1960), p. 165.
21. Ibid.
22. *From Paradise Lost to Paradise Regained,* p. 202.

We are told that God had predestinated the "requirements and the qualifications" of this heavenly class before
the foundation of the world. The number was also foreordained, but not revealed until John wrote Revelation
7:4 and 14:1-3. This amazing misinterpretation of Scripture gives exclusively to these "chosen ones" all the names
and rights given in the Bible to the saints. The 144,000
constitute the bride, the Lamb's wife. They are the elect,
the holy nation, the royal priesthood. They only are
anointed with God's spirit, and are members of the body,
the church. Designated requirements are:

1. They must exercise faith in God's provision, the shed
blood of Christ. This, of course, includes baptism, sym-
bolizing dedication. "Christ Jesus then acts as an advocate,
covering the sins of such dedicated one by the merit of his
sacrifice. The dedicated one is *now* in position to be justi-
fied or declared righteous by God, and thus he has access
to God through Christ Jesus. He has an acceptable body
and the right to perfect life on earth, and all this can be
presented for sacrifice with Christ Jesus" (LG 298-99,
italics added).

2. "God now . . . causes his active force or holy spirit to
act upon them so as to bring them forth as spiritual sons
with the hope of life in the heavens, and he acknowledges
them as his sons" (LG 300). (See above—the baptism of
Jesus.)

3. They must "demonstrate their dependability by carrying out their dedication faithfully until death" (LG 301).
"If they resist Satan and his world and maintain integrity
until death, they are assured of the 'crown of life,' immortality, divine nature" (LG 302).

The apostles were the first members of this group.

D. The other sheep are promised everlasting life on
earth. These are the unnumbered persons now working as
Jehovah's Witnesses. For them there is no suggestion of

justification or regeneration. They must have faith in Jesus Christ, preceded by repentance from sin. Then they must be baptized by immersion. This baptism symbolizes complete dedication and is a declaration of their stand for God's universal sovereignty. This "baptism into the greater Noah" saves them now, and later it will keep them saved through Armageddon, *"provided* . . . they abide in him, keeping their good conscience through faith and loyal service" (NH 311).

The Jehovah's Witness is never given a clear title to salvation. Every suggestion of assurance is qualified by the absolute requirement of continuance in faith, endurance, obedience, and witnessing.

> According to Watchtower teaching, one of four possible destinies awaits a person when he dies: (1) he may remain in the condition of non-existence into which death has plunged him (as in the case of Adam, Cain, Judas, and others beyond redemption); (2) he may be "raised" with a "spirit body," thus receiving immortality, after which he will go directly to heaven to reign there with Christ (as one of the 144,000); (3) he may be raised with a physical body and then, after having passed the millennial tests, receive everlasting life on the renewed earth; or (4) he may, after having been raised with a physical body, still fail to pass the millennial tests, and thus eventually be annihilated.[23]

THE DOCTRINE OF THINGS TO COME

It should be noted that the Kingdom of God is *entirely heavenly.* It is a Sovereign-empowered theocratic government with Jehovah himself as the great Everlasting King. Christ Jesus is co-regent, with the 144,000 as associate kings. "The term also is used to refer to the realm over which the Kingdom government exercises control" (MS 226).

23. Hoekema, p. 295.

A. In 1914 the Kingdom began operation in full with the enthronement of Christ in the heavens.

In that year Christ received his "never-to-be-destroyed" Kingdom. This marked the end of the "appointed times of the nations"[24] and the time of the end of this world began. This is proved by the following amazing compilation of Bible passages:

(1) Daniel 4:16—The "appointed times of the nations" is 7 times.

(2) Revelation 12:6, 14—A time, times, and half a time means 3½ times, or half of 7 times. 3½ times equal 1,260 days (v. 6); therefore 7 times would be 2,520 days.

(3) Numbers 14:34; Ezekiel 4:6 set God's rule as "a day for a year." Therefore, 2,520 days mean 2,520 years!

In 607 B.C. Jerusalem was captured by Babylon, to begin the "times of the nations." Proceeding 2,520 years from 607 B.C. brings us to A.D. 1914, the year in which Christ's "second coming" took place. At that time, "the devil and his angels were hurled down to earth, and all kinds of trouble ensued for the people on the earth."[25] World War I is proof of this!

B. In 1918 two major events took place:

1. Jesus entered the "spiritual temple, and began to cleanse it." This marked the period of judgment and inspection of his spirit-begotten followers—that is, the 144,000 who had died. These were now "raised with spirit-bodies to join him at the spiritual temple" (LG 203). This is the *first resurrection*. Included within this resurrection are all members of the 144,000 who die subsequent to 1918. They are given spiritual bodies immediately at death—provided, of course, that they have maintained integrity!

2. The judgment of the nations began. The people liv-

24. *From Paradise Lost to Paradise Regained*, p. 173.
25. Ibid., p. 176.

ing in the world are being divided into "the sheep and goats" (Matt. 25:31-46). The resurrected members of the 144,000 are associated with Christ as judges. The basis of judgment is the individual attitude toward Jehovah's Witnesses and their message.

C. The Battle of Armageddon is the next great event in history. It is imminent! This is "the battle of Jehovah God Almighty in which his executive officer Christ Jesus leads invisible forces of righteousness to destroy Satan and his demonic and human organization, eliminating wickedness from the universe and vindicating Jehovah's universal sovereignty" (MS 24). "Organized religion," the great harlot of Revelation 17:1-3, will lead all nations as part of Satan's organization in heaven and earth. The beast of Revelation 17:3 is the United Nations! It was (as the League of Nations), is not (during World War II), and has ascended (as the U.N.) (see Rev. 17:8).

Armageddon does not mean a literal place. Megiddo is symbolic. "Armageddon refers to God's war by which he destroys the world at the accomplished end."[26] It is said that over "two billion people will die."[27] Satan will be crushed and cast into the abyss for 1,000 years (Rev. 20:1-3). This abyss is a "deathlike state of inactivity," like the state Jesus Himself was in when He died. Thus Genesis 3:15 is fulfilled!

D. Armageddon survivors will enter the Millennium on earth. The new earth (new human society under new social arrangements) will be governed by the New Heavens (Christ Jesus and the 144,000). "There will be no evil, no disease, nor aches nor pains . . . but lasting peace and unity—one worship of Jehovah" (LG 26). Vigorous, energetic youth will be the lot of every faithful human. And Armageddon survivors will marry and have children.

26. *From Paradise Lost to Paradise Regained,* p. 204.
27. *You May Survive Armageddon into God's New World* (Brooklyn: Watchtower Bible and Tract Society, 1955),

When, according to the divine mandate, the earth is full to capacity, "people will stop having children."[28] Every child will have full opportunity for life through Christ the King but "any not desiring to serve Jehovah will be executed" (LG 269).

E. There will be two resurrections early in the Millennium. The first persons to be raised to life on earth with physical bodies will be Jehovah's faithful witnesses of pre-Christian times. These are the Old Testament faithful, such as Enoch, Noah, Abraham, David, and so forth. They will become direct children of Christ the King and will be princes on the earth. Included with them will be "other sheep" who may have died before Armageddon.

Next will be the resurrection of those who "wanted to do right, but died without opportunity to hear, or learn. . . . Decent . . . sincere people."[29] They will be taught the truth and judged according to what they do about it. If they obey God's commands, they will get life; if not, they will go to everlasting death, as Adam did. *Let God be True* optimistically states that "the greater mass of humankind will find life here on earth amid paradise conditions" (LG 279).

Noteworthy is the teaching that the Millennium is a "1,000-Year Day of Test," or judgment. "All earth's inhabitants in the new world of righteousness" will be judged. But they will not be judged on the basis of their past deeds, "but on the basis of what their deeds will be during the judgment day" (LG 293).

F. The final test, or judgment, will come when Satan, the devil, is loosed (Rev. 20:7-9). By deceit, he will gain a large following and lead a final rebellion against Jehovah. Christ the King steps aside "for the Supreme Judge, Jehovah God, to make the test" (NH 353). All the rebels, with

28. *From Paradise Lost to Paradise Regained,* p. 225.
29. Ibid. p. 229.

Satan and his demons, will be cast into the lake of fire and sulphur, Gehenna. That is, "they are disintegrated, annihilated, as if they had never existed before" (NH 355).

The issue of Jehovah's universal sovereignty will have been settled for good, forever.

G. The 144,000 having been raised in spirit-bodies, will remain in heaven for eternity. They are "joint-heirs and co-rulers" with Christ, in Jehovah's theocracy. The "other sheep" will remain on earth, entering "upon an eternity of paradisaic happiness in the ever-abiding new earth" (NH 360). "Absolute and endless destruction" is the doom of all others.

3

Sun Myung Moon's Unification Church

"WE NOW HAVE THE MEANS TO HEAL all modern-day human problems, exalt every human soul, and bring the kingdom of God within the reach of every man."[1] This all-embracing claim is based upon "new revelations from God" which were given to the Reverend Sun Myung Moon, founder of the Unification Church (The Holy Spirit Association for the Unification of World Christianity, Inc.). Briefly told, this new interpretation of the Bible teaches that God created the world of goodness to last forever. But Satan seduced Eve and brought about the Fall of man, and God's good world ended abruptly. Ever since, God has been trying to rectify His creation, but has not yet succeeded. He has worked through chosen men, His champions. All were men of self-denial, but all failed to find acceptance with men. Abel, Noah, Abraham, Jacob, Moses, yes, and Jesus Christ, they all failed. "The death of Jesus was neither his will nor his fault. . . . [It was] murder, and his body was taken by Satan" (CC 104). Having failed as He did, Jesus will come again as the Lord of the second advent. At first He will suffer and be rejected. But He will find His chosen bride; they will become the True Parents; and heaven on earth will be literally achieved.

1. Sun Myung Moon, *Christianity in Crisis* (Washington, D.C.: Holy Spirit Association for the Unification of World Christianity, 1974), p. IX (hereafter cited as CC).

THE FOUNDER

Sun Myung Moon was born in Korea on January 6, 1920. With his family members, he was "converted" to Christianity at the age of ten. On Easter morning, 1936, while deep in prayer, he had a vision. Jesus appeared to him and told him that he had been chosen to complete the mission which He had started two thousand years ago. God, it appeared, was lonely, and longed for fellowship with man.

By 1944 he had gained a following in North Korea. He was, however, badly treated by the Communist regime, and apparently he was rescued from execution by the U.N. forces in 1950. Later that year he began to teach his Divine Principle. In 1954 he officially established his new church, calling it The Holy Spirit Association for the Unification of World Christianity, or simply The Unification Church. There are shadows over certain reputed sex practices in the early days of the church, as there are over Moon's own marital affairs. However, in 1960 he was married to his present wife, who is either his fourth or second, depending on which report one believes. They have nine children.

"The union between Sun Myung Moon and Hak Ja Han is called 'The Marriage of the Lamb.' Moon is called 'the Father of the universe' and his wife is called the 'Mother of the universe.' Consequently their [nine] children are considered to be sinless. Together, the parents and children are heralding the coming perfection of humanity."[2]

SOURCES OF AUTHORITY

A. The Holy Bible is one of the Unification Church's sources of authority—but the Bible is subject to new interpretation based upon the revelations given to Mr. Moon.

2. J. Isamu Yamamoto, *The Puppet Master* (Downers Grove, Ill.: InterVarsity, 1977), p. 21.

B. *The Divine Principle*[3] is "a set of principles based on the patterns which Rev. Moon found in the Bible during his years of search" (CC 120). It is a weighty volume of 536 pages, translated into English from Korean. In it are the basic doctrines of the Unification Church. Being considered only part of the new truth, it will be enhanced as expected "deeper parts of the truth will be continually revealed." The general introduction to this book declares that

> with the fullness of time, God has sent His messenger to resolve the fundamental questions of life and the universe. His name is Sun Myung Moon. For many decades, he wandered in a vast spiritual world in search of the ultimate truth. On this path, he endured suffering unimagined by anyone in human history. . . . He fought alone against myriads of Satanic forces, both in the spiritual and physical worlds, and finally triumphed over them all. In this way, he came in contact with many saints in Paradise and with Jesus, and thus brought into light all the heavenly secrets through his communion with God [DP 16].

THE DOCTRINE OF GOD AND MAN

"God Himself told me that the most basic and central truth of this universe is that *God is the Father and we are His children*" (CC 9). God is, by definition, the creator of all things. He is the absolute reality, eternally self-existent, transcendent of time and space. However, "being the first Cause of all creation, [God] also exists because of a reciprocal relationship between the dual characteristics of positivity and negativity" (DP 24). Thus, before creating the universe, God was incomplete. He existed only as the internal masculine subject, and He created the universe as His external feminine object. This theory is obviously re-

3. Sun Myung Moon, *The Divine Principle* (Washington, D.C.: Holy Spirit Association for the Unification of World Christianity, 1973) (hereafter cited as DP).

lated to the book *I Ching*, of the Taoist religion. In it the basic fundamental of the universe is the constant interplay between the Yang and Yin (positivity and negativity).

From this comes the principle that God cannot exist without man, as man cannot exist without God. There cannot be love without a lover and a beloved. Even God needs "to share, to have give and take with someone in a reciprocal relationship. . . . That is why God created His object, man" (CC 4). Further, "God and man are one. Man is incarnate God." As such, man "is as important in value as God Himself" (CC 5).

Thus it is that man was created in the image of God in order to fulfill this need in God. And this relationship is fulfilled when man lives in full accord with the will of God, in union with God. But as God finds his joy in giving Himself in and for His creation, so He gave the pattern for the universe and for man. *We* are to live our lives for others. Thus the circle is complete. And "without this give and take action between subject and object . . . nothing endures for eternity" (CC 16). Further, heaven (the Kingdom of God) will be on earth when there is God-involvement in every human relationship. (See "SALVATION AND THE KINGDOM OF GOD ON EARTH.")

THE DOCTRINE OF THE FALL OF MAN

God had poured His soul into the creation of His masterpiece, man. He gave "100% of Himself." The circle was to be complete, each giving of himself for the other. But selfishness emerged and the circle was broken. In fact, it was never completed. Eve became Satan's first victim; then Adam was ensnared; and God was isolated in the Garden of Eden. How did it happen?

A. Lucifer was an archangel, able to "monopolize God's love as mediator between God and the angelic world" (DP 78). When God loved Adam and Eve, Lucifer resented it.

He seduced Eve, and by the act of sexual intercourse she "received certain elements from Lucifer." Eve, hoping to get rid of those elements, seduced Adam. However, she merely passed them on to him, and thus they were transmitted to all their descendants. The elements were fear, which came from a guilty conscience, and wisdom that was immature.

B. The Fall was both *spiritual,* through the blood relationship between the angel and Eve, and *physical,* through the blood relationship between Eve and Adam. In the spiritual fall, Eve submitted to Satan, and "received the elements of fear (from a guilty conscience), and wisdom enabling her to perceive that her intended spouse . . . was Adam" (DP 79). The physical Fall was caused because the relationship between Adam and Eve centered on Satan. Thus the "elements" were inherited by Adam and passed on to their descendants. Instead of the good lineage of God, the evil lineage of Satan was multiplied. This, actually, is what God has been seeking to rectify ever since. And He will, it appears, through the True Parents who will have sinless children!

God's work has been that of restoration. In seeking to destroy the world of evil and re-create the world of goodness, He needs tools. "The religions of the world have served as these tools for God." Christianity is the "most progressive religion because it teaches sacrificial love and duty in supreme form" (CC 18). The Lord of the Second Advent, who will come as the central figure of Christianity, will accomplish the ultimate purpose of all the religions.

THE DOCTRINE OF THE SAVIOR, JESUS CHRIST

The basic questions are: Who was Jesus Christ? What did He hope to accomplish on earth? Did He succeed? Will He come to earth again? Is Rev. Moon the Lord of the Second Advent?

A. Who was Jesus Christ? In *The Divine Principle,* the answer is not clear. It is stated that He was the incarnation of the Word, and that he may well be called the Creator. This means, however, that he was a man who had fulfilled the purpose of creation, and "does not signify that he was the Creator Himself" (DP 211). "As a man [Jesus was] no different from us except for the fact that he was without original sin" (DP 212).

At present He is in the spirit world as a divine-spirit-man with his disciples, but He has attained a higher level of being than they. "The fact that he called on God for help, was tempted by Satan, and finally crucified by the evil force" (DP 212) makes it clear that Jesus was not God himself. "He was the one who lived God's ideal in fullest realization" (CC 12). With this in mind, it is to be noted that "a perfected man, in light of the purpose of creation, should become perfect (Mt. 5:48); thus, he is so valuable as to even possess deity! Since God is eternal, man, who was created as His substantial object, should also become eternal, after his perfection" (DP 209). "Jesus was a man who had attained the purpose of creation" (DP 290). "In light of his attained deity, he may well be called God. Nevertheless he can by no means be called God himself" (DP 210-11).

B. Why did He come to earth? He came, as a man, to be the True Parent of mankind. He came as Messiah, to save fallen man. This means that He came to restore men as citizens of the Heavenly Kingdom. It is to be remembered that God created man for fellowship. Man was to be the means of fulfilling God in the subject-object relationship. The first Adam had failed. Jesus was the Second Adam. He was to have found His chosen bride, the Second Eve, and "to bring forth upon this earth his own sinless children. Thus the Second Adam and Second Eve would become the

True Parents for mankind, and all mankind would have found life by grafting on to them" (CC 28).

C. Did He succeed? No. In spite of the fact that the "field had been prepared" in Israel, He did not find acceptance as Messiah. He did not come to die on the cross. That was not in the predestinative will of God. In fact, Christ "prayed desperately" that it might not take place. He died "a reluctant death" due to the unbelief of the Jewish people. "His body was invaded by Satan, and he was killed" (DP 148). He failed as other champions had failed.

Mention should be made here of the dismal part played by John the Baptist in this failure. He, the expressed forerunner, was to "accomplish the mission which Elijah had left unaccomplished on earth" (DP 162). He knew that Jesus was the Messiah. But he began to doubt, and then to disbelieve. His rejection of Jesus as Messiah influenced the Jewish people to deny Jesus also.

However, the cross was not all in vain. Without it Christian history could not have existed. "We can never deny the magnitude of the grace of redemption by the cross. . . . [But] the cross has been unable to remove our original sin and restore us as men of the original nature who cannot sin" (DP 142). Nevertheless, through faith in Jesus Christ one experiences "spiritual rebirth." That is, he is saved "spiritually." The explanation is found in this quotation from *The Divine Principle:*

> As it is written (I Cor. 12:3) when we come to believe in Jesus as the Savior through the inspiration of the Holy Spirit, we receive the love of the spiritual True Parents, coming from the give and take action between Jesus, the spiritual True Father, and the Holy Spirit, the spiritual True Mother. Then, through this love, new life is infused into those who believe in Christ, and each is reborn into a new spiritual self. This is called "spiritual rebirth" [DP 216].

D. Will He come to earth the second time? Yes, He will come again as the Third Adam, the Lord of the Second Advent. He will come "in the flesh," as He did the first time. That is, He will not come in clouds of glory. At first, He will suffer many things and be rejected. Some "saints" will recognize Him, and "the Kingdom of Heaven will be first realized in their hearts." With their increase, "the Kingdom of God will gradually appear" (DP 506). This means that He will become the True Parent, and that He will thus bring about the Kingdom of God on earth.

On the basis of Revelation 7:2-4 and 14:1, it has been revealed to Mr. Moon that "Christ will be born in a country in the East—that is, from the rising of the sun—and will place a seal on the foreheads of the 144,000" (DP 520). That nation is Korea. The Korean people will become the Third Israel, "God's elect." (See DP 520-32.)

E. Is Sun Myung Moon the Lord of the Second Advent? From many angles, it would appear that he fits the picture. His birth, his revelations, his wife and family, his Unified Family (the Unification Church), his being hailed as "the Perfect Father" suggest a positive answer to the question. He is openly known as the Master, or Father. "He and his wife are the Perfect Parents who will bring salvation to the world."[4] In his book *The Puppet Master*, J. Isamu Yamamoto quotes from the *120-Day Training Manual* of the Unification Church as follows:

> By loving the Messiah [Moon] and obeying and believing the Messiah more than my own life, and by doing what he requires with great faith, now we can realize the Kingdom of God on earth and in heaven. . . . Father [Moon] is sinless, Mother [Moon's wife] is sinless, and their children are sinless. This is called the Messiah's family; this was established in 1967, on December 31. . . . Through Father [Moon] and Mother [his wife] we can be born

4. Yamamoto, p. 65.

anew, sinlessly. . . . Father is given authority here on
earth by God to forgive sins.[5]

Apparently the claim to Messiahship is not made publicly. But the "inner teachings" support the belief that Moon
is Messiah, the Lord of the Second Advent. Mr. Yamamoto
quotes further from the *120-Day Training Manual:* "Father
is visible God."[6]

It might be added that such fulfillment of the second
coming of Christ in Mr. Moon follows a pattern. There is
the accepted principle that "spirit-men . . . must come to
earth again and fulfil the responsibility they left unaccomplished in their physical life on earth through the physical bodies of earthly men" (DP 181). Elijah's return in
John the Baptist is cited as proof of this.

The Doctrine of Salvation, and the Doctrine of the Kingdom of God on Earth

A. Salvation, as *The Divine Principle* handles it, is a
complex subject. The events in the Garden of Eden caused
man to fall in two ways: spiritually and physically. Christ's
work of redemption on the cross accomplished "spiritual
salvation" for man. But it did not accomplish his physical
salvation. Original sin remained in all men. This must be
annihilated in order for the Kingdom of God to be established on earth. In *The Divine Principle* it is stated that "if
Jesus had not been crucified, he would have accomplished
the providence of salvation both spiritually and physically.
He would have established the Kingdom of Heaven on
earth which would last forever" (DP 147). The salvation
of spirit and body is called also the "providence of restoration." But Christ failed, and "even the saints redeemed by
the cross have had to continue to fight against original sin"
(DP 149).

5. Ibid., p. 54.
6. Ibid., p. 87.

Christ's coming as Lord of the Second Advent is to be with the purpose of completing His unfinished work. He must come as the True Parent. And when the "True Father and True Mother become one, and love each other, God would come down and become one with them on earth."[7] Because God is spiritual only, he creates a central person, or persons, through whom mankind can receive rebirth. The True Parents give spiritual life. And this is presently realized "by loving the Messiah [Moon] and obeying and believing the Messiah more than my own life, and by doing what he requires with great faith."[8]

The "doing what he requires" is related to restoration through indemnity. This is a complex matter "revealed" at length in *The Divine Principle*. "The providence of restoration cannot be fulfilled by God's power alone, but it is to be fulfilled by man's joint action with God" (DP 283). This spells *works* and explains somewhat the hours spent by the "Moonies" as they sell flowers in public places. Testimonials tell of days that start at 5:00 A.M. and rarely end before midnight. In addition, "we must first establish direct rapport with God in spirit through ardent prayer, and next, we must understand the truth through correct reading of the Bible" (DP 152). This latter point may account for the seemingly interminable public and private lectures to which the young followers are subjected.

B. It is taught that bodies are only temporal dwellings for spirits. The human body, once it is corrupted and decomposed, cannot be resurrected into its original state. Further, "it is not necessary for a spirit man to resume his flesh, when there is a vast spirit world where he is supposed to go and live forever" (DP 170).

Therefore, resurrection means the phenomena occurring

---

7. Frederick Sontag, *Sun Myung Moon* (Nashville: Abingdon, 1977), p. 119.
8. Yamamoto, p. 54. Quoted from the *120-Day Training Manual*, p. 328.

in the process of man's restoration, according to the providence of restoration, from the state of having fallen under
Satanic dominion, back to the direct dominion of God.
Accordingly, when we repent of our sins, making ourselves better and better, day by day, we are coming closer
to resurrection [DP 170].

In brief, there is no physical resurrection. The resurrected Jesus was not the Jesus who had lived with His disciples. He was a being transcendent of time and space.
He had given up His physical body as a sacrifice.

By devious means, it is explained that "spirit men who
passed away to the spirit world without having perfected
themselves . . . must come again to earth and fulfil the responsibility they left unaccomplished in their physical life
on earth through the physical bodies of earthly men, by
cooperating with earthly saints and helping them fulfil the
same mission" (DP 181). John the Baptist and Elijah "co-
operated" to fulfill the mission Elijah left unaccomplished!

C. There is an elaborate hierarchy of attainment by
which men will achieve entrance into the Kingdom of
Heaven on earth. Fallen man must be raised to a proper
relationship with God by the providence of restoration.
This "perfection" is to be accomplished through three or-
derly stages of growth; the form-spirit stage, the life-spirit
stage, and the divine-spirit stage. Until the time of Jesus,
men attained the form-spirit stage after death by having
kept the Law. Since the cross, men attain the life-spirit
stage (and go to paradise) through faith in the gospel (DP
175). During the time of the Lord of the Second Advent,
"spirit men of this age can attain the divine-spirit stage of
perfect restoration by believing and serving the Lord of
the Second Advent" (DP 175).

Regardless of one's position (stage) in the spirit world,
he can raise his spirit level by intercommunicating with
men on earth. There must be active give and take between

spirit and body in order to produce intermediate and ultimate fulfillment—that is, in order that the divine-spirit stage might be attained and the Kingdom of Heaven reached. "The ultimate purpose of God's providence of restoration is to save all mankind" (DP 190). Hell is a temporary condition, and is in the world. Paradise is likewise a temporary dwelling place inhabited by men of the life-spirit stage as they await the opening of the Kingdom of Heaven. That kingdom is as yet vacant.

D. In Moon's writings, much is said about the Kingdom of Heaven, or Kingdom of God, on earth. It should have been established by Jesus when He came the first time. As we have noted, He failed, but He will succeed when He comes again. Then, men will live in union and communion with God, the True Parent. God will be living for men, and men for God. There will be God-involvement in every relationship. The so-called Four Position Foundation—God, husband, wife, offspring in perfect give-and-take relationship—will be the base through which God's power will be channeled into all creation.

Marriage is believed to be essential to this salvation. Only the male and female together can represent God totally. The marriage relationship is therefore advocated in the Unification Church. "In February, 1975, Moon married 1800 couples in Seoul, Korea, from twenty-five countries."[9] "The matching was done by the Master [Moon] and many of the couples hardly knew or had ever seen each other before.[10]

Another facet is added to this by the revelation to Moon that the Holy Spirit is a female. "She came as the True Mother, that is, the Second Eve" (DP 215). "She also cleanses the sins of the people in order to restore them, thus indemnifying the sin committed by Eve" (DP 215).

9. Yamamoto, p. 55.
10. Sontag, p. 167.

As noted above, attainment of a place in the kingdom would appear to be guaranteed to all mankind. It will be a world (on earth) in which God's commands will be conveyed to all His children through the True Parents, and all will work toward one purpose.

The True Parents play a significant role in this. It is frequently indicated that Jesus will come as the Third Adam (Lord of the Second Advent). He will take a bride. The marriage supper of the Lamb will take place. All mankind will find life by being "grafted" into his family.

Mr. and Mrs. Moon are now being called the True Parents. They and their nine children are sinless, and are the beginning of the Kingdom of Heaven on earth.

The earth will be populated by divine-spirit beings living in perfect harmony with God. Thus in the give and take between subject and object, the perfect relationship will be maintained. God will be completely fulfilled in His creation.

❀   ❀   ❀

As a postscript, it is interesting to note that the American president of the Unification Church, Neil Albert Salonen, is quoted as saying that the theology of the church is "still evolving. That's not to say we don't know what we believe, but Rev. Moon is still receiving revelations."[11] He further added that in 1977 the church had an estimated income of $24.7 million. The church owns $20 million worth of property in New York state, half of which is mortgaged. "Members who sell candy and flowers gross an average of $80 per day from sales, and this is the main source of income for the church."[12]

11. In *The Christian Reader,* September-October 1978, p. 34.
12. Ibid.

4

Herbert W. Armstrong's Worldwide Church of God

THE WORLDWIDE CHURCH OF GOD owes its beginning and continuance to its founder, Herbert W. Armstrong, and to his son, Garner Ted Armstrong. Born in 1892, Herbert W. Armstrong's particular interest in the Bible began in 1924. A neighbor lady had persuaded Mrs. Armstrong to keep the Sabbath. Herbert W. was motivated to frantic study to prove her wrong. This experience led him out as a preacher with a variety of church groups. Ultimately, in January 1934, the Radio Church of God came into being. This became the Worldwide Church of God. Amazing growth has been fostered by intense salesmanship via publications, radio, and television. Some five hundred local congregations are claimed, with membership represented as 75,000. "The World Tomorrow," the church's television program, claims an audience of 30 million. Radio programs over more than three hundred stations reach additional millions of people. Financially, the "fabulous take" is reported as some $75 million a year. Circulation of the church's monthly magazine, *The Plain Truth* (sent without charge to all who ask for it), is around 2 million. It is published in five languages in 187 countries. The Ambassador College Correspondence Course is available on the same free basis.

Garner Ted Armstrong has been the "silver-tongued spokesman," during recent years, on radio and television.

In 1972 Herbert W. "yanked" Garner Ted off the air and sent him into exile. No reasons were given. Insiders later reported that the son was guilty of adultery. Garner Ted had been head of the church and of the church-owned Ambassador College. Some time later, he was reinstated, but he was again excommunicated by his father in June 1978. This was apparently final.

The ousted son has formed a new church, The Church of God International, apparently hoping to draw dissidents from his father's domain. News media suggest a power struggle as being a major factor in the rift, with a financial crisis aiding further separation. There has been as yet no indication of any significant defection toward the new church.

The Worldwide Church of God (Armstrongism) has no equal as an example of extreme eclecticism coupled with a blatant claim to originality. "The prophecies and mysteries of God, sealed until now, are today revealed to those whom God has chosen to carry His last message to the world as a witness."[1] There is only one true church of God. "All others are counterfeit."[2] And yet it is clearly observable that basic doctrines of the Worldwide Church of God are similar to those of the Jehovah's Witnesses, Mormonism, et al., and certainly British-Israelism is not unique to Armstrong.

The basic theory of British-Israelism is that the Anglo-Saxon countries, Britain and its former empire (including the United States), are the ten lost tribes of Israel. In brief, note these points:

1. God's promise to Abraham was that he should be the father of many nations, of whom the Jews were only one.

1. Herbert W. Armstrong, *The Book of Revelation Revealed at Last* (Pasadena, Calif.: Ambassador College Press, 1959), p. 4.
2. Herman L. Hoeh, *A True History of the True Church* (Pasadena, Calif.: Ambassador College Press, 1959), p. 28.

2. God made an "unconditional and unbreakable" covenant with David. The throne of David was to be established forever (2 Sam. 7:13). This throne exists today.

3. Israel lost its identity in 721 B.C., when its people were carried away captive to Assyria, and became known as "the ten lost tribes."

4. Ephraim, which according to Jacob's prophecy was to become a multitude of nations (a commonwealth), is Great Britain.

5. Manasseh is the United States.[3]

Added is the fantasy that the Scottish Stone of Scone (which is placed under the throne in Westminster Abbey) is actually the stone used by Jacob as a pillow at Bethel. It was taken by the prophet Jeremiah to Britain when he took the daughter of Zedekiah to Ireland. Thus Elizabeth II is Queen of Israel! The Saxons (Isaac-son), or British (*Brit* being Hebrew for "covenant" and *ish* meaning "*man*"), are the covenant people!

In the Worldwide Church of God the only recognized source of authority is the Bible. The only true interpretation is that of the Worldwide Church of God.

THE DOCTRINE OF GOD

God is the creator, the beginner, the one who caused us to have life, and so is called our Father.[4] However, declaring the doctrine of the Trinity to be pagan and false, the Worldwide Church of God emphasizes that "God is a Family, a Kingdom, NOT a limited trinity."[5] Further, "at the present time there are only two beings in the God Family.

---

3. Herbert W. Armstrong, *The United States and the British Commonwealth in Prophecy* (Pasadena, Calif.: Ambassador College Press, 1954).

4. David Jon Hill, "Why Is God the Father Called a Father?" *Tomorrow's World,* September-October 1970, p. 24.

5. *The Plain Truth.* August 1958, p. 17.

1) God the Father, Father of Jesus Christ, 2) God of Abraham, Isaac, and Jacob, the One who became Jesus Christ, God the Son."[6] However, on the basis that God is reproducing Himself, men are actually begotten (not born) as sons at conversion. As they grow spiritually, they will be "born of God" at the time of the resurrection. For "man was created to literally become God."[7] And "we shall one day be . . . divine as He is divine."[8] To emphasize this further, it is written that we shall actually "generate eternal life intrinsically within ourselves" and "will counsel and advise our Creator-Father."[9] It should be noted that this partakes of Mormon doctrine, but seems to go to a greater extreme.

THE DOCTRINE OF CHRIST

"Christ has existed from all eternity with the Father. He is one with the Father, but He is subordinate to the Father."[10] The Yahweh (Jehovah) of the Old Testament is Jesus Christ.

Jesus Christ, Yahweh, became man, being born of the virgin Mary. Until that time, He was not the Son. Armstrong's Ambassador College Bible Correspondence Course says:

> Before Christ (the Logos) was conceived in Mary, He was not the "Son of God." He was one of the two original members of the God Kingdom. He, like the one who became the "Father," had existed eternally. But He is nowhere in God's Word referred to as a Son of God prior to His conception in Mary. His human birth was His first birth.[11]

6. "The God Family," *Tomorrow's World*, May 1971.
7. Robert L. Kuhn, "What It Means to Be Equal with GOD," *Tomorrow's World*, April 1971, p. 43.
8. Herbert W. Armstrong, *What Do You Mean—Born Again?* (Pasadena, Calif.: Ambassador College Press, 1962), p. 15.
9. Kuhn, pp. 44-45.
10. Paul N. Benware, *Ambassadors of Armstrongism* (Nutley, N.J.: Presby. & Ref., 1975), p. 44.
11. Ambassador College Bible Correspondence Course, lesson 8.

As a man, He could have sinned, but did not. He "became perfect through the trials and tests of human experience.... He kept God's commandments perfectly, . . . [and] developed the perfection of spiritual character which enabled Him to become our Savior and elder brother."[12] He died as a voluntary sacrifice on the cross to pay the penalty of sin. However, as will be noted later (see "THE DOCTRINE OF SALVATION"), "the blood of Christ does not finally save any man."[13]

Crucified on Wednesday (as is adamantly maintained by Armstrong), Christ was raised again on Saturday, at the end of the Jewish Sabbath. But note that "the resurrected body was no longer human—it was the Christ resurrected, immortal, once again changed! . . . He was . . . converted into immortality, and He is alive forevermore."[14] Having been given immortality, He was now a spiritual Son of God, a divine Being. As to the body, it disappeared.[15] Presumably, in dying, Christ ceased to exist. He was then re-created by God after three days of total extinction.

(Concerning the doctrine of the Holy Spirit, it should be noted that His personality is denied. "The Holy Spirit is the very power of God. *It* expresses the unified, creative will of the God family."[16] In similarity to Jehovah's-Witness teaching, "the Holy Spirit is not a third person of the Godhead as taught by the pagan 'trinity' idea."[17] Note also that God is *not* omnipresent. "The Father and the Son are in definite locations . . . the spirit proceeds from them

---

12. Ibid., lesson 9.
13. Herbert W. Armstrong, *All About Water Baptism* (Pasadena Calif.: Ambassador College Press, 1972), p. 2.
14. Herbert W. Armstrong, "Why Christ Died—and Rose Again," *The Plain Truth,* April 1963, p. 10.
15. C. Paul Meredith, *If You Die—Will You Live Again?* 1958, 1971, p. 6. Quoted by R. L. Sumner, *Armstrongism* (Brownsburg, Ind.: Biblical Evangelism Press, 1974), p. 113.
16. Ambassador College Bible Correspondence Course, lesson 9.
17. Ibid.

and fills the entire universe."[18] "Whenever we become members of God's begotten family, we receive a portion, a seed or germ, of the Father's Holy Spirit."[19])

THE DOCTRINE OF MAN

The account of creation is accepted literally. The creation of man "in the image of God" took place approximately six thousand years ago. The Fall of man was planned and permitted by God. Any other explanation would suggest that Satan outwitted God.

"In its view of man the Worldwide Church of God adopts the view of conditionalism, along with the Seventh-Day Adventists and Jehovah's Witnesses. Conditionalism teaches that man was created as a living soul with the potential for immortality."[20] Holding thus to the teaching of "conditional immortality," the Worldwide Church of God teaches that the condition of all men after death is that of unconsciousness, or "soul sleep." They remain thus until the resurrection of the righteous to immortality and life, and of the unrighteous to annihilation.

THE DOCTRINE OF SALVATION

To begin, it is interesting to note that Jesus alone, of all humans, has so far been saved![21]

A. "Salvation is by faith in Jesus Christ by which one is enabled to keep the Law. Acceptance of Christ cleanses from past sins, but justification will be given only on condition that the Law is kept."[22] Thus it is that salvation is a process. And it promises no certainty until the resurrection. One who is born of God is "merely begotten spir-

18. Herbert W. Armstrong, *How You Can Be Imbued with the Power of God* (Pasadena, Calif.: Ambassador College Press), p. 5.
19. Ibid., p. 4.
20. Benware, p. 102.
21. Herbert W. Armstrong, *Why Were You Born?* (Pasadena, Calif.: Ambassador College Press, 1957), p. 11.
22. Herbert W. Armstrong, *What Kind of Faith Is Required for Salvation?* (Pasadena, Calif.: Ambassador College Press, 1952).

itually." He is "not yet really born." Only those who develop spiritually "shall finally be given immortality—finally changed from mortal to immortal at the time of the second coming of Christ."[23]

B. Baptism by immersion is an absolute essential. "There is no promise that anyone will receive the Holy Spirit until baptized in water."[24]

C. The keeping of the Law includes:

1. *Sabbath observance.* "To break God's Holy Sabbath is sin, and the penalty is eternal death."[25]

2. *Annual feast days.* They are: the Passover, during which set time the Lord's Supper is observed; Seven Days of Unleavened Bread, which follow the Passover; Pentecost, which symbolizes the coming of the Holy Spirit; Feast of Trumpets; Day of Atonement (Yom Kippur), which pictures the future day when "the responsibility for sin will be placed on the head of Satan, the devil"—Satan is the scapegoat![26]

3. *The Ten Commandments.* The second commandment, relating to graven images, is interpreted as excluding all idolatrous church festivals, such as Christmas, Easter, New Year's Day, Lent, and so forth—even birthdays! The seventh commandment, "Thou shalt not commit adultery," means that only a first marriage is valid. Divorce is sinful, for whatever cause. Any marriage subsequent to divorce is adultery. However, it is understood that there has been a softening of the attitude of the Worldwide Church of God in this regard.

4. *Dietary regulations.* The dietary regulations of Leviticus 11 and Deuteronomy 14 are mandatory, as are the de-

23. Armstrong, *All About Water Baptism*, p. 2.
24. Ibid., p. 8.
25. Herbert W. Armstrong, *Which Day Is the Sabbath of the New Testament?* (Pasadena, Calif.: Ambassador College Press, 1952), p. 56.
26. K. C. Herrmann, *God's Sacred Calendar, 1970-71* (Pasadena, Calif.: Ambassador College Press, 1970), p. 11.

cisions of the Jerusalem Council of Acts 15. Smoking is a
sin, but drinking alcoholic beverages is not.

(It might be noted here that "Sickness is only the penalty of physical transgression, and whenever one is sick,
he is paying the penalty. Healing is nothing more or less
than the forgiveness of sin. God is the only real physician!
Scripture labels other modes of healing idolatry. Medicine has a pagan origin."[27] Armstrongism advocates the
laying on of hands and anointing with oil for healing.
Tongues-speaking is denounced as being of the devil.)

5. *Tithing.* Tithing is a major emphasis, with "free-will
offerings." In practice, this includes a first tithe, second
tithe, third tithe, and so on. Instances are quoted of members who give 30-40 percent of their income to the church.

D. However, "a majority of those who die without
Christ will be resurrected and gain opportunity to believe
during the Millennium."[28]

THE DOCTRINE OF THINGS TO COME

"According to Armstrong, the year 1972 should have
ended the work of God and brought in the events of the last
days (1934 to 1972 completes the two nineteen-year time
cycles.) This has caused Armstong some prophetic problems."[29] Nevertheless, the introduction to lesson 4 of the
Correspondence Course declares that "no other Bible
course in this world even dares to reveal the future as does
this Course; . . . this Work really understands Bible prophecy."[30]

A. We are now in the last days, which precede the Tribulation—the time of Satan's wrath. The Tribulation will
last three and one-half years and will be followed by the

27. Herbert W. Armstrong, *Does God Heal Today?* (Pasadena, Calif.:
    Ambassador College Press, 1952), p. 8.
28. Herbert W. Armstrong, *Predestination—Does the Bible Teach It?*
    (Pasadena, Calif.: Radio Church of God, 1957).
29. Benware, p. 66.
30. Ambassador College Bible Correspondence Course, lesson 4.

time of God's wrath. This is the sixth seal of Revelation 6:12-13. During this time, apparently, the "faithful" will be supernaturally transported to Petra, the ancient rock-walled city on Edom. There they will be protected from the horrors going on in the world. The time of God's wrath is the beginning of the Day of the Lord, which climaxes in the second coming of Christ.

B. At the Battle of Armageddon, the hosts of wickedness will be destroyed by the returning Christ. At the same time, the first resurrection will take place. The "dead in Christ" will rise and, together with the "living," will be changed from mortal to immortal. After rising to meet the Lord, they will immediately descend with Him to rule over the millennial earth. Satan will be bound, and the 1,000 years of peace and prosperity will ensue.

C. The second resurrection will involve those who never really had a fair chance to hear the truth. This is the judgment of the great white throne. "Isa. 65:20 indicates those resurrected at that time will live for a hundred years."[31] The Gospel will be explained, but Satan "will be ... allowed freedom to deceive the nations again."[32] It is hoped that most will believe the truth and be converted. All who do not will be cast into the lake of fire.

D. The third resurrection follows immediately after the judgment of the great white throne. "This handful of recalcitrant sinners will be annihilated—cast into the Lake of Fire. The Father will then move his throne to earth, and the earth will become the eternal center of the universe."[33]

E. Heaven apparently is reserved for the Father and His angels.

31. Herbert W. Armstrong, *If You Die, Will You Live Again?* (Pasadena, Calif.: Ambassador College Press), p. 7.
32. Herbert W. Armstrong, *What Is Satan's Fate?* (Pasadena, Calif.: Ambassador College Press), p. 4.
33. Joseph Hopkins, *The Armstrong Empire* (Grand Rapids: Eerdmans, 1974), p. 97.

Christ will reign on earth throughout eternity.[34] "The Earth, and a definite, specific location on the earth, will be where Jesus said He is going to be. If we are to be with Him where He is to be—then we, also, are going to be on this earth."[35]

Hell, sheol, hades, and *the lake of fire* all appear to be considered synonymous terms. "The wicked will be resurrected at the close of the Millennium, but only to be annihilated."[36] Acknowledging that Jesus spoke of "the fire that never shall be quenched" (Mark 9:43), the Worldwide Church of God teaches that the fire "will burn itself out, when the wicked and all their wicked works are burned up."[37] Satan and his angels, however, being spirit beings, "will be tormented unto the ages of ages. . . . The exact nature of their eternal punishment is yet to be determined."[38]

34. Ibid.
35. Herbert W. Armstrong, *Will You Get to Heaven?* (Pasadena, Calif.: Ambassador College Press), p. 11.
36. Herbert W. Armstrong, *Lazarus and the Rich Man* (Pasadena: Radio Church of God, 1953).
37. Herbert W. Armstrong, *What Is This Place Called Hell?* (Pasadena, Calif.: Ambassador College Press), p. 18.
38. Armstrong, *What Is Satan's Fate?*, p. 7.

5

The Way International

"THE WAY INTERNATIONAL is a biblical research and teaching organization concerned with setting before men and women of all ages the inherent accuracy of the Word of God (the Bible) so that everyone who so desires may know the power of God in his life. The Way is not a church, nor is it a denomination or a religious sect of any sort."[1] This is the introductory declaration in an attractive, multicolored pamphlet entitled *This Is The Way*. Its terminology is essentially that of evangelical Christianity. It offers, reputedly for a fee of $100, study classes focusing on power for abundant living. Capitalizing on the discontent and enthusiasm of youth, The Way International purports to give new light on the Scriptures. This new light is the outcome of over thirty years of biblical research and teaching by its founder and president, Dr. Victor Paul Wierwille.

The Doctor, as he is called by his followers, studied at the University of Chicago and at Princeton Theological Seminary, where he was awarded the Master of Theology degree. His doctoral degree is from Pike's Peak Bible Seminary, a reputed degree mill. For sixteen years he served as a pastor in northwestern Ohio with the Evangelical and Reformed Church, later known as the United Church of Christ. He resigned his pastorate in Van Wert, Ohio, in 1957 to begin his present activity.

1. *This Is The Way* (New Knoxville, Ohio: The Way, Inc., International, n.d.).

The heart of his "new light" on the Scriptures is presented in four volumes which make up *Studies in Abundant Living*. The style is disparaging of much orthodox biblical interpretation. Dogmatic and critical, the Doctor is not slow to write that nothing is so dynamically thrilling as the inherent accuracy of God's wonderful, matchless Word, and to indicate that he has the only true interpretation. "The Word of God is the Will of God. It means what it says and says what it means."[2] And he, the Doctor, is the one who knows what it means!

"God," he testifies, "spoke to me audibly, just like I'm talking to you now. He said He would teach me the Word as it had not been known since the first century, if I would teach it to others."[3] God later give him a sign in confirmation of the voice. In response to his request, God sent snow. One moment the sky was crystal and clear. He closed his eyes. When he opened them, he testified, the "sky was so white and thick with snow I couldn't see the tanks at the filling station on the corner not 75 feet away."[4] He later received the "holy spirit," and spoke in tongues. "The holy spirit field—that's the field God raised me up for. . . . And there's no one I can't lead into speaking in tongues if they are Christian and want to do it."[5]

The Way International has been characterized as combining biblical literalism, evangelicalism, Calvinism, ultra-dispensationalism, and Pentecostalism.[6] Wierwille uses Scripture extensively to prove teaching that is far from orthodox. His use of Hebrew and Greek, with appropriate explanations, is impressive (as it is no doubt intended to be).

2. Victor Paul Wierwille, *The Word's Way,* Studies in Abundant Living, vol. 3 (New Knoxville, Ohio: American Christian Press, 1971), p. 229 (hereafter cited as WW).
3. Elena S. Whiteside, *The Way: Living in Love* (New Knoxville, Ohio: American Christian Press, 1972), p. 178.
4. Ibid., p. 180.
5. Ibid., p. 201.
6. J. M. Hopkins, "The Word and the Way According to V. Wierwille," *Christianity Today,* September 26, 1975, p. 42.

The Structure of The Way is likened to that of a tree. "Leaves and twigs, branches, limbs, trunk, and roots. Each statewide unit is a limb, each city unit a branch, each household fellowship group a twig, each believer a leaf."[7] The leaf becomes "rooted and grounded and established" in knowledge and practical application of the Word in the "twig."

THE SOURCE OF AUTHORITY

The one and only recognized source of authority is the Bible. But it is the Bible as distinctively reinterpreted by the founder. A strong dispensational view indicates that the "church began with Paul's Epistles. The Gospels belong in the Old Testament; and only those New Testament Epistles addressed to the church apply to believers today—although the remainder of the Bible is 'for our learning.' "[8] *The Way Magazine* of September-October 1974 declares that "the Pauline epistles are absolutely flawless, divine revelation. . . . In the Gospels we do not see the ministry of the Lord Jesus Christ at the right hand of God. . . . The gospels give only a sense-knowledge acquaintance of the Lord Jesus Christ." Further, "the so-called Christian Church today is built essentially on man-made doctrine, tradition, confusion, bondage trips, and contradiction to the Word as it was originally 'God-breathed.' "[9]

THE DOCTRINE OF GOD

Elohim, God alone, is Creator of heaven and earth. The Way, like the Jehovah's Witnesses, categorically rejects any suggestion of Trinitarian doctrine. Such teaching is relegated to religion that began in the time of Nimrod. The plural word *Elohim* (as in Gen. 1:1) is simply indicative of supremacy and lordship, the plural of majesty. (An

7. *This Is The Way.*
8. J. L. Williams, *Contemporary Cults (The Way)* (Burlington, N. C.: New Directions Evang. Assoc., n.d.), p. 8.
9. *The Way Magazine,* September-October 1974, pp. 3, 7.

interesting note on Genesis 1:28 states that the command to replenish the earth indicates that prehistoric man antedated Adam and Eve.)

THE DOCTRINE OF JESUS CHRIST

A. Jesus Christ is not God. In 1975, Wierwille wrote a book with this title. Enlarging upon material already published, it is a bold and acknowledged disagreement with orthodox Trinitarian doctrine.

1. Jesus was not coexistent with God, either in spirit or any other form. "God is eternal whereas Jesus was born. Matthew 1:18" (WW 26). On the declared basis that God was alone from the beginning, it follows that God is the "Word" of John 1:1. This verse is interpretatively corrected to read: "In the beginning was the Word [God] and the [revealed] Word was with God" (WW 28, brackets are Wierwille's).

2. The created Word (Jesus Christ) was with God *in His foreknowledge*. God, being spirit, had to find means to manifest Himself "in concretion." He gave the revealed Word so that man might be able to understand His communication. The revealed Word refers to both the written Word (the Bible) and the created Word (Jesus Christ). It is interesting to note that "we the chosen of God were called in Him in His foreknowledge," in the same way that Jesus Christ was with God "in His foreknowledge" (WW 29).

B. Jesus Christ was a perfect man. Wierwille adamantly declares that Jesus is the "Son of God, but not God." "He was a specially created, perfect man whose body came from Mary and whose soul or 'life Principle'—manifested as 'blood'—was specially created by God in Mary's womb."[10] Christ is presented as having been uniquely created by a form of divine insemination so that He was born sinless.

10. Williams, p. 9.

"Jesus Christ's existence began when He was conceived by God's creating the soul-life of Jesus in Mary. God created, brought into existence, this life in an ovum in Mary's womb" (WW 37). John 1:13 is cited as proof of this. This verse refers, according to the Doctor, not to the believer, but to Christ. "He was born (begotten) NOT OF BLOOD. . . . The only one who did not partake as a natural man in the life of the flesh, which is in the blood, was Jesus Christ" (WW 37). In *Jesus Christ Is Not God*, Wierwille interprets Hebrews 2:14 as indicating that Jesus only "took part, not all" of Adam's flesh and blood. "The life of the flesh in the blood of Jesus came by way of supernatural conception by the Holy Spirit, God."[11]

Other Scriptures which demonstrate the deity of Christ are brushed aside by reinterpretation. John 10:30 reads "I and my Father are one." Wierwille holds that this means simply that they were "one in purpose." He makes no mention of the violent reaction of the Jews who heard the statement. They certainly took his meaning to be more than oneness of purpose! Hebrews 1:2 is taken to mean that the worlds were made *for* the Son, not by the Son. Likewise Ephesians 3:9, which is translated to read, "all things were created by (on account of, or for) Jesus Christ."

C. Wierwille maintains the dogmatic position that Christ was crucified on Wednesday and was raised seventy-two hours later on Saturday afternoon. This teaching is not unique. Numerous evangelicals concur with this view. The founder-director of The Way had further light, however, on the events of that day. He takes strong, and lengthy, exception to the teaching that Jesus actually carried the cross. There is "no record" of this, he says. The cross was borne all the way by Simon, the Cyrenian. "The unlearned man has made the cross of Jesus a wooden cross.

11. Victor Paul Wierwille, *Jesus Christ Is Not God* (New Knoxville, Ohio: American Christian Press, 1975), p. 71.

The Word says, and the spiritual man knows, that Christ's cross was sin, bondage, sickness, and pain. A wooden cross could not accomplish anything, but the cross of Jesus did much" (WW 227). A point incidental to this: "Wierwille concurs with the Witnesses and with Armstrong in the teaching that the victims died upon stakes rather than crosses."[12]

There were four men crucified with Christ—two thieves and two malefactors. This contention is largely based on the use of different words by Matthew and Luke. "The two malefactors (*duo kakourgoi:* [Luke 23:32-33]) were crucified at the time Jesus was crucified, while the two robbers (*duo lēstai* [Matt. 27:38]) were crucified later" (WW 240). Making considerable use of the niceties of New Testament Greek, Wierwille exalts his own ability to "read accurately and to study what is written."

Another notable rejection of accepted orthodox teaching changes the translation of the Aramaic words "Eli, Eli, lama sabachthani?" (Matt. 27:46). These words were uttered by Christ while on the cross, and are commonly rendered, "My God, my God, why hast thou forsaken me?" Wierwille's translation is "My God, my God, for this purpose was I spared, for this purpose was I kept, for this purpose came I into the world, for this purpose was I reserved" (WW 273). He makes no mention of Psalm 22:1, from which these words were actually quoted.

The Doctrine of Redemption

A. Redemption is by faith in Jesus Christ. Any Jew or Gentile who confesses Jesus Christ as his Lord and believes that God raised Him from the dead is born again and is a member of the body of Christ. "He has Christ in him, the hope of glory." This will be recognized as evangelical truth. It must, of course, be tempered by the realization

12. Hopkins, p. 40.

that the essential deity of Christ is denied. And without the deity of Christ, there is no adequate atonement.

In *Jesus Christ Is Not God*, Wierwille felt it necessary to fulminate on this point. "Trinitarian dogma," he writes, "degrades God from his elevated, unparalleled position; besides, it leaves man unredeemed."[13] Further, "if Jesus Christ is God and not the Son of God, we have not yet been redeemed."[14] In this, the founder of The Way rejects the truth that Jesus Christ is the God-man, the perfect sacrifice and perfect substitute for sinful man.

B. Salvation includes deliverance from the power of darkness. That is, "when we have salvation, we have wholeness, even physical wholeness if we simply accept it."[15] Complete healing from any sickness or disability is available to all believers. Apparently this is not a matter of extreme emphasis. When asked to tell of "some fantastic healings," the Doctor answered, "I don't remember too many specific healings. You see . . . healings and miracles are a result of the Word of God living in a person's heart . . . by-products of the Word."[16]

C. Wierwille differentiates between the bride of Christ and the body of Christ. "The kingdom of heaven period is for the called-out (ekklesia) of Israel, the church of Israel, which is the bride of Christ" (NDC 7). This is the church of the period of Law and of the gospels. It will also be the church of the book of the Revelation, at which time the bride and groom will be together. On the other hand, the body of Christ began on the Day of Pentecost and continues until the return of Christ. During that period, "every one who is born again by God's Spirit is a member of the Church of Grace, the body of Christ" (NDC 10). Al-

13. Wierwille, *Jesus Christ Is Not God*, p. 85.
14. Ibid., p. 6.
15. Victor Paul Wierwille, *The New, Dynamic Church*, Studies in Abundant Living, vol. 2 (New Knoxville, Ohio: American Christian Press, 1971), p. 31 (hereafter cited as NDC).
16. Whiteside, p. 169.

so called the Church of God, it includes both Jewish and
Gentile believers.

The Doctrine of the Holy Spirit and of "holy spirit"

Wierwille distinguishes these terms, with vehemence.
His contention is that God *is* Holy Spirit. (This, of course,
accords with his anti-Trinitarian position.) "And since
God is Holy Spirit, He can only give what He is—holy
spirit" (NDC 103). Whenever God the giver is referred
to as the Holy Spirit, Holy Spirit is always capitalized.
His gift, holy spirit, is not.

A. An individual receives holy spirit when he is saved.
This gift of holy spirit has nine parts, or manifestations,
as listed in 1 Corinthians 12. All of them are received by
all believers, including the gift of speaking in tongues.

B. "There's no one I can't lead into speaking in tongues,
if they are Christian and want to do it."[17] In pursuance of
the conviction that "the holy spirit field" is one distinctive
for which God has raised him up, Wierwille urges every
believer to exercise this gift. The experience of so doing
is the "overflow" of the spirit, and it edifies the body of
believers.

Speaking in tongues may be both in private and in public. In the first case, it is for prayer and praise, and is never
interpreted. In the second, it is for edification, and must
be interpreted. Apparently it is not uncommon for a period
of such "manifestation" to be programmed into public
meetings. An individual might pray by request, or by demand. It is emphasized that "what you say when you speak
in tongues is God's business, but that you *do* speak is your
responsibility" (NDC 109). Instructions are precise and
clear. "I am ministering the holy spirit to you. . . . Close
your eyes and sit quietly" (NDC 122). "Believe to be natu-

17. Ibid, p. 201.

ral and at ease. You have to move your lips, your throat, your tongue; you push the air through your voice box to make the sounds" (NDC 117-18). "Just breathe in. Open your mouth wide. While you are breathing in, thank God for having filled you with the fullness of the power of His holy spirit. . . . Speak forth. When you have finished one sound, speak another. Do not pay any attention to what you are thinking. . . . You formulate the words . . . You are magnifying God no matter what the words sound like to your ears. It is your part to speak in tongues; it is God's part to give the utterance" (NDC 123).

Conclusion

Wierwille's writings are voluminous, and they are characterized by a personally distinctive exposition of Scripture. His writing style is extremely dogmatic, with interpretations that are frequently at odds with orthodoxy. A typical expression is "It simply isn't so," with reference to commonly accepted teaching. Not all his views are heretical by orthodox standards. While Christ's deity is denied, His birth, miracles, death, resurrection, and ascension are accepted as biblical truth. Regeneration is considered essential, and that by faith in Jesus Christ, God's Son. Eternal life, received at the moment of faith in Christ, can never be lost.

Wierwille's major emphasis upon "Power for Abundant Living" carries acceptability by many in this day of lowering standards of Christian holiness. He has applied Christian teaching to the whole man in all of life. Apparently this makes an appeal to many unsatisfied young people and others who are dissatisfied with the lifelessness of many churches.

6

Hinduism-based Movements

THE INVASION OF THE WESTERN HEMISPHERE by Eastern
mysticism is not new. Literary men have thought that
New England transcendentalism of the nineteenth century
was influenced by Hinduistic philosophy. Christian Science and Theosophy are basically Hindu in essential teaching. However, the primary impact, as Hinduism, was
probably made in the United States at the Parliament of
World Religions, in 1893. The news media expressed ad-
miration for the brillance of the Swami Vivekananda, the
representative of Hinduism. Heeding the pleas of many
who heard him, he conducted a number of seminars
throughout the land. As a result, the teaching of the Vedanta was established at several urban centers. Vedanta
(meaning the "end" or "ultimate" in knowledge) is ex-
pounded in the Hindu scriptures called the Vedas. The
teaching emanates principally from the Upanishads (c. 600
B.C.), supplemented by the Bhagavad Gita (Song Celestial,
c. first century of the Christian era). The word *Upanishads*
has various meanings, but carries the connotation of "secret
doctrine," or "that which dispels darkness or ignorance
completely."[1] The understanding is that those who attain
Knowledge are emancipated from the bondage and darkness of ignorance. Having become one with the divine
(Brahman), they will no longer be subjected to the pangs
of reincarnation.

1. Charles Samuel Braden, *The Scriptures of Mankind: An Introduction*
(New York: Macmillan, 1952), p. 111.

94

It is fascinating to note that the main concern of the ancients was to explain how man relates to ultimate reality. Their solution lay in the realization that common man is ignorant of his own true nature. "Not moral transgression but mental error is the root of human misery and evil."[2] As non-dualistic Vedanta explains it:

> Brahman (the ultimate Reality behind the phenomenal universe) is "one without a second." Brahman . . . is consciousness. Brahman . . . is existence. Brahman is the . . . Eternal Nature of every human being, creature, and object. . . . Life has no other purpose than this—that we shall learn to know ourselves for what we really are.[3]

In the Upanishads the repeated declaration is, "That art thou!" The ultimate and infinite Reality, and you, are one and the same!

This is the teaching called monism, the "great discovery" of India's sages. It maintains that the superficial ego-personality which claims individual existence is unreal and transient. The fundamental principle is that man, in his real nature, is divine; and the purpose of human existence is the realization of this divinity within oneself. This is also called the perennial philosophy; it is claimed to be the eternal religion, the highest common factor of all religions. The goal, then, is God-realization, which is really self-realization. *Enlightenment* is a synonymous term. While it is a mystical experience, it is essentially experiential—it radically changes one's life-style now, and it also determines the eternal future.

This teaching is enhanced in the Bhagavad-Gita, the Song Celestial of the Lord Krishna. Three facets are basic: First, the soul of man is immortal, a part of the beginningless and endless creation. "There never was a time when I did not exist, nor you, nor any of these kings, nor is there

2. John B. Noss, *Man's Religions* (New York: Macmillan, 1956), p. 229.
3. Christopher Isherwood, ed., *Vedanta for Modern Man* (New York: Collier, 1962), p. 9.

any future in which we shall cease to be."[4] Second, the soul, or man, is eternally a part of the Infinite, the Absolute, the Brahman, the only Reality. Third, reincarnation (transmigration) and karma (the law of the deed, the law of cause and effect) explain life as man sees it. Successive reincarnations (reputedly averaging 8,400,000) are the steps by which the individual soul climbs upward to become *one* with the Infinite. It is then freed from the "illusion" of individuality and enters into its rightful position of eternal life, infinite wisdom, and abiding happiness.

"Vedanta has one great peculiarity: it declares that there must be no attempt to force mankind to travel one path; but that we must allow infinite variation in religious thought, knowing that the goal is the same."[5] Thus wrote Swami Prabhavananda in *Vedanta for Modern Man*. It will be noted later that several of the modern movements tend to claim uniqueness in being "the only way," or having the "authentic technique." This is not in keeping with the historic teaching of the Vedanta.

A commonly accepted doctrine within the Hindu system is that the "teaching" (whatever its emphasis might be) has been transmitted through the ages by men who have "realized deity." Each of these, usually designated "guru" (teacher) or "Guru Dev" (Divine Teacher), taught his chosen disciples. At times the light would seem dim, but it would constantly reappear in and through one of these "great souls." Names such as Shankaracharya (the great exponent of non-dualism), Ramanuja (the great exponent of modified non-dualism), or Madhavacharya (the great exponent of dualism, which holds that men are separate individual personalities even after liberation) are well known to students of the Vedanta. The "gurus" of today consistently refer to their teachers from whom they re-

4. Swami; Prabhavananda and Christopher Isherwood, trans., *Bhagavad-Gita: Song of God* (New York: Mentor Classic, 1951), p. 36.
5. Isherwood, *Vedanta for Modern Man*, p. 30.

ceived enlightenment. Thus the Guru Maharaj Ji acknowledges his father, Shri Hans Ji Maharaj, as his Satguru; Guru
Maharishi Mahesh Yogi learned the technique of transcendental meditation (TM) from his teacher, Guru Dev; His
Divine Grace A. C. Bhaktivedanta Swami Prabhupada
teaches the supremacy of the Lord Krishna, as he learned
from his guru, Bhakti Siddhanta Sarasvati; and so on. None
of the present "swamis" claims originality, although each
indicates that his is *the* way for the present time.

Of the currently active "gurus," the young Maharaj Ji is
blatantly hailed as "Lord of the Universe," the "greatest
incarnation of God that ever trod the face of this planet."
Among a number of parodies on Bible verses, the one relating to Matthew 6:33 reads, "First of all one should have
Knowledge from Guru Maharaj Ji and afterwards all the
accessories will be added to him."[6] However, His Divine
Grace, A. C. Bhaktivedanta Swami Prabhupada, of Iskcon,
is presented as "one who knows the Absolute Truth." He
is to be honored as highly as the Supreme and Mighty Lord,
for "he is the great God's most confidential servitor." This
is frequently emphasized in the movement's publication,
Back to Godhead.

"The Upanishads preach that the best way of purifying
the heart is through contemplation and meditation, . . . an
unbroken stream of thought focused on an object."[7] Thus,
meditation is a common facet of Hindu systems. And the
mantra is likewise central in the practice of meditation.
Webster defines it as "a verbal spell, ritualistic incantation,
or mystical formula used devotionally in popular Hinduism
or Buddhism." It may be individually assigned by a teacher, as in TM; or all devotees may use the same mantra, as
in Iskcon. But the purpose is to "still the mind," to attain

6. Charles Cameron, ed., *Who Is Guru Maharaj Ji?* (New York: Bantam, 1973), p. 277.
7. Isherwood, *Vedanta for Modern Man*, p. 294.

perfect calmness. Such is preliminary to the ultimate state
of "spiritual reality."

There is no suggestion of atonement for sin Sin is more
the absence of good, and it is offset by one's own devotion
to his chosen path to salvation. At any rate, the outwork-
ing of the law of karma is absolutely inexorable. Good will
be rewarded; nongood will be punished. Since Christ is
generally hailed as one of the great divine gurus of the
past, it is claimed that one may accept the present guru
without rejecting Christ. They are really teaching the
same truth, according to the Vedantic view. As the Maharishi observes, "the crest of Vedic wisdom . . . is the essence of Christianity, essence of Buddhism, essence of Islam, essence of any life."[8]

Transcendental Meditation

Transcendental Meditation (TM) is undoubtedly the
most insidious of current movements. Defined as "a path
to God" by its founder and leader, it is propagated as "nonreligious." As such, it is fostered by several state govern-
ments, and financed by public funds. "The Vedas [Hindu
Scriptures] provide a direct technique to cognize . . . that
all-pervading reality, almighty God" (M 21). That technique is TM. "Just learn to meditate; go within and experience the Divine Nature" (M 158). But, having thus
declared his message and purpose, the astute founder recognized that the religious message is not attractive to many
in the sophisticated West. So he capitalized on a statement from the popular Hindu scripture called the Bhagavad-Gita. There the Lord Krishna says, "Let not him
who knows the whole disturb the ignorant who knows only
a part." Therefore, TM meets the ignorant on the level of
his ignorance. "Very few souls are there in the world of
today who would go for God alone" (M 169).

8. Maharishi Mahesh Yogi, *Meditations of Maharishi Mahesh Yogi*
(New York: Bantam, 1973), p. 66 (hereafter cited as M).

TM's appeal is the claim to improve the quality of life; to develop the full potential of mind and body; to enjoy fulfillment of life. According to the Maharishi, man is already divine. He needs no savior.

Maharishi Mahesh Yogi graduated from Allahabad University, in India, and subsequently studied for thirteen years with his "swami," Guru Dev (Divine Teacher). The Yogi (meaning that he has attained union with the divine) began his movement in the United States in 1959. As of 1976, TM claimed to have more than half a million Americans who were trained in its technique, more than two hundred SIMS (Student's International Meditation Society) centers in the United States, one thousand chapters on college campuses, five thousand instructors in the United States and Canada, and twenty thousand new trainees every month. More recent figures indicate a decline, perhaps occasioned by a number of law suits which challenge TM's nonreligious status. The Society of Creative Intelligence (SCI) is the theoretical aspect of TM. The SIMS is the banner under which TM gains access to schools and colleges. The Spiritual Regeneration Movement (SRM) is perhaps the most evidently truthful of TM's subtitles. The Maharishi does say that TM "meets man on the level of man and transforms him to the Divine" (M 91-92). Maharishi International University, established in 1974 in Fairfield, Iowa, integrated the teaching of SCI into its four-year degree program.

The key to this technique of meditation is the mantra. By means of the individually assigned mantra, the mind of the practicer is drawn to the "deepest and most refined level of thinking." That is the "divine nature" which is in every man. The realization of this innate divinity automatically brings freedom from any oppression of guilt or from depression caused by the "darkness of ignorance." Surely there is no less demanding, easier way to supreme bliss!

(See M 90-93.) In TM, a mantra is simply *a group of sounds.*
The effectiveness is in the sounds themselves. The mantra
is usually short, and it is to be repeated silently over and
over again as the medi†ator sits in a comfortable position
with eyes closed. This he is to do for fifteen to twenty
minutes twice daily. By it, his mind is "drawn towards its
subtler stages until it reaches its own essential nature" (M
183). Incidentally, the mantra must never be spoken aloud
or revealed to any one, else it will lose its effectiveness.

How does one receive his own personal mantra? The
process usually begins with one or two free lectures. The
trained instructor pointedly declares that TM is nonreligious. It is *not* contemplation or concentration. It is not
a spiritual or philosophical experience. It is simply a technique for deep rest and relaxation. It does not involve with-
drawal from life. Upon payment of a required fee ($55 for
high school students, $65 for college students, $125 for
working adults) the initiate receives instruction. During
each of these private sessions, the instructor analyzes "the
quality of energy impulses of the individual . . . and selects
the mantra" (M 9). It is a "special sound whose vibration
influences produce all good, congenial, favorable, valuable
effects on the outer life" (M 184). The Maharishi under-
lines that the silent sound of the repeated mantra must
"rightly correspond to the energy impulses of the man, . . .
or it is sure to create unbalance in the harmony of the man's
life. . . . This is the main strength of the Spiritual Regeneration Movement" (M 185-86).

After the instruction and analysis, and prior to receiving
the personal mantra, the initiate *must* be present at a "puja"
ceremony. *Puja* is the Hindi word commonly used in North
India to indicate Hindu idol worship. (It is not used by
Christians living in India.) Although the would-be meditator is told that he need not participate, he *must* attend.
He must bring six flowers, three pieces of fruit, and a white

handkerchief, which are to be offered before the image of Guru Dev. The ritual is conducted in Sanskrit, the ancient language of India, the language in which the Hindu scriptures were written and which is used today as the Hindu priests intone their mantras and their puja of the gods. The trained TM instructor recites the required ritual, having learned it by rote. "Even the physical movements which accompany the recitation are choreographed in detail, and carefully memorized."[9] But SIMS instructors are hesitant to describe frankly the details of the ceremony to prospective meditators The reasons are obvious.

The first of the three stages of the ritual begins with the invocation "To Lord Narayana" and progresses through a sequence of references to historical and legendary personages until it reaches Shri Guru Dev. He, of course, is the immediate teacher of Maharishi, the founder of TM.

During the second stage, some seventeen items are offered before the image of Guru Dev, the Divine Master. Each offering is accompanied by the words "I bow down." The flowers, fruit, and handkerchief brought by the initiate are individually placed upon the altar. The puja concludes with a hymn of praise and adoration to Shri Guru Dev. He is addressed as "Guru in the glory of Brahma; Guru in the glory of Vishnu; Guru in the glory of the great Lord Shiva . . . to Him I bow down."[10] He is the one by whom "the blinding darkness of ignorance has been removed." Incidentally, Brahma, Vishnu, and Shiva make up the supreme triad of the gods of Hinduism.

A former TM instructor wrote the following about his experience: "At the end of the song, the teacher indicates to the person to kneel for a few moments of silence, and then, both still kneeling, the teacher repeats the mantra selected for the person, and has him repeat it until he has

9. *An English Translation of Transcendental Meditation's Initiatory Puja* (Berkeley, Calif.: Spiritual Counterfeits Project, n.d.), p. 1.
10. Ibid., p. 2.

it correctly pronounced, and then they are seated for further instruction. Many candidates I encountered while teaching TM objected to this religious aspect, but went along with it in order to learn the technique."[11] Another writer adds: "At the end of the puja, the teacher actually bows before the altar. Simultaneously, he makes a carefully rehearsed gesture towards the candidate which invites him to bow down beside his initiator."[12] Failure to comply disqualifies one from TM. During subsequent lessons, participants practice meditation, discuss their experiences in groups, and are then on their own.

It is claimed that the result is "a deep state of rest," "reduction of anxiety and emotional disturbances," "inner alertness," "reduced dullness and improved efficiency in perception and performance," and "more energy for purposeful activity."[13] The uniqueness of such claims has been disputed. It has been scientifically demonstrated that similar results ensue from other methods of meditation.

However, assuming that the practicer attains such results, is that all there is to TM? Pressed for an answer to this question, an instructor confessed, "The advanced TM meditator would find within himself a depth of power unimaginable." For TM is only a beginning, a gradual movement from matter to mind, and then to supermind. This final attainment is explained as being "union with the Divine," the "glorious Cosmic Consciousness," the realization of the self, which is the impersonal god who is in every man, being, and object. *This* is the purpose of TM. It is a subtle method of captivating the ignorant on the level of his ignorance. It offers peace without a Savior. No need of such, for the source of power is within. This do-it-your-

11. David Haddon, *Transcendental Meditation: A Christian View* (Downers Grove, Ill.: InterVarsity, 1975), pp. 9-10.
12. Myra Dye, "The Transcendental Flimflam," *Moody Monthly*, January 1975, p. 34.
13. *Scientific Research on T.M.* (Los Angeles: Maharishi International University Press, 1972), pp. 1, 3, 6, 7, 9.

self formula has greater appeal than the message of repentance from sin and faith in God's Son.

The Maharishi's planned deception in presenting TM as nonreligious has enjoyed remarkable success. The number of trainees reached a peak of 40,000 a month in 1975. Federal grants have been given for the teaching of TM in public schools in California and in New Jersey. The house of representatives of the state of Illinois resolved that "all educational institutions be strongly encouraged to study . . . courses in TM and SCI." However, in 1976 a nationwide Coalition for Religious Integrity (spearheaded by the Spiritual Counterfeits Project of Berkeley, California) filed a federal lawsuit to stop classes in TM techniques in four New Jersey high schools. The suit was successful. *Christianity Today* reported that the ruling was that "the defendants have failed to raise the slightest doubt as to the facts or as to the religious nature of the teachings."[14]

TM monthly enrollments slid to a low of 4,000 in 1977. News media suggested that this may have led to a "new advance" in the program. Teaching is being offered which costs up to $5,000. It purports to give "the ability to walk through walls, . . . become invisible, . . . [or] hover in midair and fly around the room." It leads finally to "actual mastery of the sky, flying at will." One enrollee expressed the hope that he will "eventually walk through a wall," but the technique he wants most is omniscience and knowledge of other planets. This is not out of line with the fundamental teaching that the deity is actually within every man. A final word in the report indicates that no demonstrations have yet been given, and that reporters are notably skeptical.[15]

GURU MAHARAJ JI AND THE DIVINE LIGHT MISSION

"I have not come to establish a new religion. I have

14. *Christianity Today*, November 1977, p. 56.
15. *Time*, August 8, 1977, p. 75.

come to reveal the truth."[16] With these words, the youthful guru places himself in succession with Jesus, who "gave Knowledge," and with Krishna, who "gave Knowledge." In the book entitled *Who Is Guru Maharaj Ji?*, printed in 1973, the Guru is presented as the incarnate Lord of the Universe, the Perfect One! He is "the greatest incarnation of God that ever trod the face of this planet" (GMJ 9). His father, it is claimed, was recognized by thousands of Indian devotees as Satguru, the one living master who reveals the ancient Knowledge of the inner self. Prior to his death, in 1966, he offered "full prostration to the Lotus Feet of his youngest son" (GMJ 11). Maharaj Ji was thus the chosen descendant of the Satguru, "crowned with the crown of Ram and Krishna . . . to take the Knowledge to the world" (GMJ 12).

The key word in the Guru's teaching is obviously *Knowledge*. That is, Knowledge by which we "can experience infinity within our own bodies" (GMJ 17). Apparently this is to approximate the ancient Hindu Gyan Marg, or Way of Knowledge. Some two thousand trained disciples, called "mahatmas," meaning "great souls," are able to transmit the "experience" to earnest seekers of truth. They teach four techniques of inner meditation known as "Light," "Music," "Nectar," and "the Word." A Knowledge session usually lasts about six hours, and "there's really something to see, hear, taste, and feel." First, "by the grace of Guru Maharaj Ji," the devotee sees Divine Light, the "sun which is within ourselves . . . brighter than the sun you see in the sky." The "third eye" is opened, and the divine light of creation is seen "inside his head." As the devotee meditates on this, he "become[s] one with God." It should be mentioned that the Guru equates God (Brahma) with per-

16. Charles Cameron, ed., *Who Is Guru Maharaj Ji?* (New York: Bantam, 1973), p. 13 (hereafter cited as GMJ).

fect and pure energy (GMJ 20-21). Second, "in the Knowledge session, we are shown how to turn our hearing sense inward to experience an actual music, the essence of every sound in the universe" (GMJ 21). Third, the Taste of Nectar, the River of Life, "is the 'ambrosia' or 'Fountain of Youth' explorers have traveled to find, not knowing it lay right inside them." "Advanced saints and yogis can live on nectar alone, as Jesus did during his forty days in the wilderness (GMJ 22). The fourth session deals with the Word, "the primordial vibration that underlies everything in existence." "In and of itself this one Word is the one reality, the illogical yet undeniable 'first cause' of the universe. The universe itself." "This is the Word. This is God" (GMJ 23).

Specific details concerning the receiving of "Knowledge" are not related. Instead, it is generally stated that it can only be experienced, not fully described. It is clear, however, that faith in the Divine Guru and dedication to him are requisite. The Knowledge can only be transmitted by touch. "If you can't get this Knowledge outside," declared the Guru, "come to me and I will give it to you" (GMJ 249). Devotees (called "premies," from the Hindi word *prem*, meaning "love") are advised to meditate upon the light, harmony, nectar, and holy Word in a quiet place for an hour in the evening and an hour in the morning. They are urged to continue to attend the nightly sessions held in any of the urban information centers and to spend time in service for others.

The Divine Light Mission movement experienced a continuing setback in 1975. The Guru's mother, reportedly disgusted with her son's "playboy" life-style, announced that she had ousted Maharaj Ji as leader of the movement and awarded the title to one of his brothers. In spite of very little publicity during recent years, the "mission's 1.2

million adherents throughout the world have remained
faithful to Maharaj Ji."[17]

HARE KRISHNA

"Once I was searching, but now I search no longer. I
am completely satisfied with Krishna. By chanting the
names of God, and living a life free from lusts, I will eventually become part of God." This testimony of an attractive sari-clad American girl illustrates the teaching of
what is popularly called the Hare Krishna movement—the
International Society for Krishna Consciousness (ISKCON).
Chanting the names of God, especially the "Supreme Personality of the godhead, Lord Sri Krishna," is the way back
to "our original blissful life." *Back to Godhead,* the colorful
magazine of the Hare Krishna movement, proclaims an essential root connection with the Vedanta. It is "the only
magazine in the Western world to present the authorized
transcendental science of God-realization known only to
the saints of India's unbroken disciplic succession."[18]

This movement is an example of the ancient Hindu way
of devotion (the Bhakti Marg). According to it, one deity
or manifestation of god is chosen to be the sole object of
devotion or worship. Krishna is actually considered to be
one of nine incarnations of the god Vishnu the Preserver,
who is one of the members of Hinduism's great triad of
gods. However, in ISKCON it is taught that "Krishna is
the Supreme Personality of Godhead and the supreme authority on the Gita, and He initially delivered the Gita so
that all persons could reach the perfection of life and be
liberated from all suffering" (BG 36:2). It is further
claimed that "Krishna consciousness is the perfect process
for solving all the problems of life because it can at once
end our illusory separation from Krishna, the Supreme

17. *Newsweek,* March 8, 1976, p. 14.
18. *Back to Godhead,* no. 36, p. 2 (hereafter cited as BG, followed by the
    issue number and the page number—BG 36:2, for example).

Lord" (BG 47:1). Krishna is the essence of all existence, and "is present everywhere, even within the atom and within the heart of every living creature" (BG 47:1). Our eternal consciousness of Krishna is covered by a cloud of forgetfulness. This cloud is dissipated by the chanting of the Mahamantra (the great mantra). This mantra, used by all devotees, is:

> Hare Krishna, Hare Krishna,
> Krishna, Krishna, Hare, Hare,
> Hare Rama, Hare Rama
> Rama, Rama, Hare, Hare

All problems are solved simply by chanting Krishna.

This is the message of the movement. Singular and simple as it is, it is a method of self-purification by "ecstatic absorption in God-consciousness twenty-four hours a day." The chanting of the mantra will cleanse the heart of all "contaminated dust and garbage." "Chant Hare Krishna and be happy," is a recurring saying. The ultimate, of course, is to "become part of God," as the young lady quoted above indicates. This is "self-realization," the "re-establishment of our lost relationship with the Supreme Personality of Godhead" (BG 47:7). It should be noted that the name *Rama* chanted in the mantra indicates the god Rama of Hinduism. He is another of the incarnations (avatars) of the great god Vishnu. Apparently, apart from inclusion within the mantra itself he gets little attention from the Krishna devotees.

The founder and spiritual master of the movement is known as His Divine Grace A. C. Bhaktivedanta Swami Prabhupada, an awesome title by which he is always addressed. But he is "the representative of Krishna," a self-realized soul who "as all scriptures reveal, should be honored as highly as the Supreme and Almighty Lord, for he is the Great God's most confidential servitor" (BG 36:26).

The principal scripture of ISKCON is the Bhagavad-Gita, in which Krishna is the supreme authority and speaker. The Gita, most popular of Hindu scriptures today, is contained within the massive Mahabharata, an epic story of a great war in India's long history.

ISKCON is a variant of the usual Vedantic invasion of the West in that it reveres Srila Madhavacharya rather than the honored Shankaracharya. Shankaracharya advocated the advaita, nondual, monistic teaching. "Madhavacharya always stressed that God and man are separate individual personalities even after liberation, and thus his philosophy is known as dvaita, or dual" (BG 36:3). Nevertheless, ISKCON includes "absorption into God," or "becoming part of God," as the highest attainment in eternity. With reference to a Bhagavad-Gita class, it "is stated in The Nectar of Devotion: Persons who are impelled by pure devotional service in Krishna Consciousness and who therefore go to see the Deities of Vishnu in the temple will surely get relief from entering again into the prison house of a mother's womb" (BG 36:15). This is tantamount to a declaration that reincarnation is no longer necessary. One has become "part of God."

The personal lives of the Krishna disciples are examples of disciplined continence. Men shave their heads, except for the Hindu *chutiya,* the usually small tuft of hair toward the back of the head. Women wear the beautiful and modest Indian saris. Eating is strictly vegetarian, as in orthodox Hinduism. Food is always presented to the deities first, and, indeed, every activity is "for the Supreme Lord." Sex is voluntarily given up, except for the purpose of having children in marriage. The dedication to Krishna is total.

Back to Godhead, the title of the magazine of the movement, indicates the proud purpose. Above the magazine name, in the front cover of each issue, the basic philosophy is declared, "Godhead is light, nescience [ignorance] is darkness. Where there is Godhead there is no nescience." Chanting the name of Krishna dispels the ignorance and reinstates the soul in the deity.

The communal lives of these young devotees of this form of Bhakti-yoga are scrupulously regulated. At 3:30 A.M. on an average day, the students are awakened by the chanting of Hare Krishna. Each day is filled with activity. Notable are Sankirtan (public chanting of Hare Krishna), printing the literature written by the spiritual master, and worship of the deity in the temple. "By His mercy the Lord appears in the Deity form of stone or wood." These grotesque idols are "bathed and dressed and fed," every morning at 4:30, in ISKCON Boston (BG 36:14). The Sankirtan party usually continues the "ecstatic chanting" and distribution of literature some six or seven hours a day. This "distribution of Krishna consciousness to the living entities who have forgotten Krishna is a far greater service than the patchwork of material welfare work, altruism, etc." (BG 36:17). The ISKCON publications are the work of the founder; they are mostly translations with explanation of Hindu scriptures pertaining to Krishna. The format usually gives the text in Sanskrit, which is followed by the transliteration in roman letters. Synonyms are explained, the translation is given, and finally the "purport," or teaching, is given. The work is largely unintelligible to an average reader. Yet people are persuaded to buy, moved by the fervent sales talk of the devotees. The devotees have made themselves obnoxious in numerous public places by their methods of persuasion, often considered illegal.

The founder and spiritual master of the movement, Swami Prabhupada, died in 1978. His decease has not produced any notable change in the activities of the devotees. Hindu dress, however, has apparently given way to a more

casual Western style among those whose assigned duties
relate to meetings with the general public.

OTHER HINDUISM-BASED MOVEMENTS

Propagated with less flamboyance are numerous other
Hinduism-based movements in the West. The Self-Realization Fellowship (SRF), founded by Swami Yogananda,
has international headquarters in India. It has its SRF centers in Europe and in the United States. Its message is essentially that of the others mentioned. True happiness is
offered as the disciple "learns the divine nature of his being." The SRF method is the Hindu Karma Marg, the
Way of Works. Concentration techniques are imparted
only on the pledge that information will not be given to
others.

The Vedanta Society is an arm of the RamaKrishna Mission. The one who organized this movement was Swami
Vivekananda, who made a great impact during the Parliament of World Religions in Chicago, in 1893. The Vedanta Society also has centers throughout the Western
world, with more than a dozen in the United States. Each
center is an independent, self-sustaining unit which is governed by its members, with a monk in charge. He usually
holds the traditional title of "swami." Literally meaning
"lord," the title indicates that he has undergone training
and has attained unto the enlightening experience which
is the ultimate in the Vedantic teaching. Generally, no ad-
vertising is done, although the notice of public meetings
will usually be found among weekend church notices in
cities where the Society operates. There will be classes on
the Upanishads and Bhagavad-Gita. The message of the
Vedanta Society is thoroughly in keeping with its name.
That is, the message is in keeping with books classified as
Vedic literature. Brahman is the only reality. Men are
caught in the illusion of ignorance. The Vedas give the

knowledge that will free the individual from bondage and release him into the Infinite.

Besides these, there are "swamis," "enlightened beings" who operate independently. Message and techniques are essentially the same, with variants that are always permissible in the Vedanta. Concentration, contemplation, and meditation with the focus within oneself: it is *there* that the *Power* lies. Go deeper and deeper into yourself; plumb the depths of your own inner being, from matter to mind, and then to supermind. Thus we reach union with the Divine. That, according to the mystical systems of the East, is Sat-Chit-Anand—Truth, Consciousness, and Bliss!

7

Christian Science

"IN THE YEAR 1866, I discovered the Christ Science or divine laws of Life, Truth, and Love, and named my discovery Christian Science. God had been graciously preparing me during many years for the reception of this final revelation."[1] The system therefore embodies a revelation for which Mrs. Mary Baker Eddy had been prepared. She claimed that her teachings and healings were definitely connected with those of Jesus of Nazareth and that her doctrine simply revealed the law by which He performed His healings. This law, until it was revealed to her, had been lost since the time of Christ. "Our Master . . . practiced Christian healing, . . . but he left no definite rule for demonstrating this Principle of healing and preventing disease. This rule remained to be discovered by Christian Science" (SH 147:24-29).

Mary Baker was born at Bow, New Hampshire, on July 16, 1821, into a devoutly religious family. Her poor health, which seems to have been a characteristic of her life, led to experiments with various types of healing. She experienced a good deal of unhappiness. Her first marriage (to George Glover) was a happy one, but it ended with the death of her husband a few months before their first child

1. Mary Baker Eddy, *Science and Health with Key to the Scriptures* (Boston: Trustees under the will of Mary Baker Eddy, first published in 1875), p. 107, lines 1-6 (hereafter cited as SH, followed by the page number and line number).

was born. In 1853 she married an "amorous dentist," Dr. Daniel Patterson. He was unfaithful, and she divorced him in 1866. In 1877 she became the wife of Asa Gilbert Eddy, "the first student publicly to announce himself a Christian Scientist."[2]

In the meantime her health continued poor, and in 1862 she resorted to a man named Phineas P. Quimby. He had been healing sicknesses reportedly without medicine. He called his system "the Science of Christ," and she apparently was convinced that he had rediscovered the methods of healing practiced by Christ. Later, however, she repudiated any indebtedness to Quimby, claiming "I won my way to absolute conclusions through divine revelation, reason, and demonstration. The revelation of Truth in the understanding came to me gradually and apparently through divine power" (SH 109:20-23).

This "discovery" came in February 1866, a short time after Quimby's death. She undertook a healing ministry and taught her system to pupils, each of whom paid a fee of $300. In 1875 she completed the book *Science and Health with Key to the Scriptures.* On August 23, 1879, the Church of Christ, Scientist, was incorporated in Boston. Its stated purpose was to "transact the business necessary to the worship of God."[3] However, the Christian Science *Church Manual* states that the purpose of the new church was "to commemorate the word and works of our Master, which should reinstate primitive Christianity and its lost element of healing."[4] Christian Science, like Mormonism, claims to be the true Christianity restored after many centuries.

2. Russell P. Spittler, *Cults and Isms* (Grand Rapids: Baker, 1962), p. 50.
3. Edwin F. Dakin, *Mrs. Eddy, the Biography of a Virginal Mind* (New York: Scribner's, 1930), p. 151.
4. The Christian Science *Church Manual*, 89th ed. (Boston: Allison V. Stewart, 1915), p. 17.

SOURCES OF AUTHORITY

"As adherents of Truth, we take the inspired Word of the Bible as our sufficient guide to eternal Life" (SH 497: 3-4).

"In following these leadings of scientific revelation, the Bible was my only textbook. The Scriptures were illumined; reason and revelation were reconciled, and afterwards the truth of Christian Science was demonstrated. No human pen nor tongue taught me the Science contained in this book, *Science and Health;* and neither tongue nor pen can overthrow it" (SH 110:13-20).

The sources are two: the Holy Bible and *Science and Health.* The second, since it is the interpretation and explanation of the first, is the final authority. The true meaning of the Bible is known only through *Science and Health,* which is said to be the "voice of Truth to this age, and . . . [a book] uncontaminated by human hypotheses" (SH 456: 27-28; 457:1-2).

The Bible as we have it is unreliable, containing many mistakes, according to *Science and Health.* These mistakes are manifest "in the ancient versions." There are thirty thousand different readings in the Old Testament, and three hundred thousand in the New, so that "these facts show how a mortal and material sense stole into the divine record" (SH 139:15-19). In another place, Mrs. Eddy was reported as saying that "the material record of the Bible, . . . is no more important to our well-being than the history of Europe and America."[5]

The title of the second authority explains its contents. *Science and Health* is a volume of more than seven hundred pages. The chapters begin with random Scripture quotations, which give the author a springboard from which to leap into metaphysical thinking. *The Key to the*

5. Mary Baker Eddy, *Miscellaneous Writings, 1883-1896* (Boston: Allison V. Stewart, 1910), p. 170.

Scriptures begins on page 501, with excerpts from the first and last books of the Bible. Sample readings are:

> Genesis 1:1—In the beginning God created the heaven and the earth.
>
> The infinite has no beginning. This word *beginning* is employed to signify *the only,*—that is, the eternal verity and unity of God and man, including the universe. The creative Principle—Life, Truth, and Love—is God. . . . This creation consists of the unfolding of spiritual ideas and their identities, which are embraced in the infinite Mind and forever reflected [SH 502:22—503:3].
>
> Genesis 1:6—And God said, Let there be a firmament in the midst of the waters. . . .
>
> Spiritual understanding, by which human conception, material sense, is separated from Truth, is the firmament [SH 505:4-8].
>
> Revelation 21:1—And I saw a new heaven and a new earth: for the first heaven and the first earth were passed away. . . .
>
> . . . St. John's corporeal sense of the heavens and earth had vanished, and in place of this false sense was the spiritual sense, the subjective state by which he could see the new heaven and the new earth, which involve the spiritual idea and consciousness of reality. . . . This is indeed a foretaste of absolute Christian Science [SH 573: 19-28].

The chapter entitled "Recapitulation" should be read as an illustration of the ambiguity and contradiction that totally encompasses this strange system which is much more Hindu than it is Christian. The introductory paragraph declares that "absolute Christian Science pervades its statements, to elucidate scientific metaphysics" (SH 465:4-6).

Two fundamental "truths" must be *ever* in mind in any study of Christian Science. Actually these "truths" invalidate and render needless *any* discussion. All subsequent study *must* relate to these absolutes. The first is this: "God is All-in-all" (SH 113:16). The second is this: "God, Spirit, being all, nothing is matter" (SH 113:17). In her *Miscellaneous Writings,* Mrs. Eddy wrote: "Here also is found the pith of the basal statement, the cardinal point in Christian Science, that matter and evil (including all inharmony, sin, disease, death) are *unreal.*"[6]

The Doctrine of God

"God is incorporeal, divine supreme, infinite Mind, Spirit, Soul, Principle, Life, Truth, Love" (SH 465:9-10).

"God is infinite, the only Life, substance, Spirit, or Soul, the only intelligence of the universe, including man" (SH 330:11).

A. The reasoning of the Christian Scientist is based on the dogmas that God is All-in-all, and is wholly good. It is repetitiously emphasized in *Science and Health* that God is all that *really is.* There is absolutely no other reality. Whatever is not God is unreal, unsubstantial, nonexistent, and the result of "mortal error." Since the majority of men do not share in the "revelation of Divine Science," they live in ignorance. This ignorance is notably seen in the "false" belief that there are other realities. Christian Science demands that men accept this concept of the allness of God in its absolute, extreme meaning. They must give up any claim or idea that there is any separateness or individuality. The individual must submerge his feeling of individuality in the determined realization that he is one with the All-in-all. When questions were raised in the attempt to bring this concept within reach of human understanding, they were either ignored or brushed aside as irrelevant. They were the outcome of the "error of mortal mind."

6. Ibid., p. 27.

When asked if God is a personal being, Mrs. Eddy answered by equivocation.

> In Christian Science we learn that God is definitely individual, and not a *person*, as that word is used by the best authorities, if our lexicographers are right in defining *person* as especially a finite *human being*; but God is personal if by *person* is meant infinite Spirit.[7]

She made no clear affirmation or denial of God's personality. It is impossible to secure an unqualified answer in simple language. For instance, it is written that "God is individual and personal." But the statement does not stop there. It continues, "in a scientific sense, but not in any anthropomorphic sense" (SH 336:32–337:1). What is a "scientific sense"? This is not explained. In addition, having denied that God is personal "in any anthropomorphic sense," Mrs. Eddy nevertheless spoke of God in anthropomorphic terms. God hears, sees, knows, and loves. Further, the use of the term "individuality," is not meant to imply that God has a form. God is "the infinite, and divine Principle of all being, the ever-present I AM, filling all space, including in itself all Mind, the one Father-Mother God."[8]

The concept of God is a very hazy one. A person who is included in and inseparable from all that is (although there is actually nothing that is apart from God) is beyond human comprehension. The impression given is that God is an impersonal being, if such is possible. The follower of Mrs. Eddy could not possibly have any concept of God as the creator who has a loving interest in His creation. The sustained denial of the existence of any material or physical creation eliminates any such possibility. The refusal to admit the actuality of sorrow or suffering obviates any partic-

7. Mary Baker Eddy, *Rudimental Divine Science* (Boston: The trustees under the will of Mary Baker Eddy, 1908), p. 2.
8. Ibid., pp. 3–4.

ular need for help from an outside source, even if such did exist.

The Trinity is repudiated in the statement: "The theory of three persons in one God (that is, a personal Trinity or Tri-unity) suggests polytheism, rather than the one ever-present I AM" (SH 256:9-11).

B. The claim that God is all that really is carries with it the obvious meaning that there is nothing else apart from from Him. Therefore Mrs. Eddy defines matter as "made up of supposititious mortal mind-force" (SH 310:5). "The objects cognized by the physical senses have not the reality of substance" (SH 311:26-27). "Firmament" in Genesis 1:6 is really "spiritual understanding." The "dry land" of Genesis 1:10 illustrates "the absolute formations instituted by Mind" (SH 507:2). "Water" symbolizes the "elements of Mind" (SH 507:3). Creation consists of the unfolding of spiritual ideas and their identities" (SH 503:1-2).

This teaching that "oneness" is the essential principle of all being was prevalent in the ancient East. *Monism* is the word used to describe the discovery of this oneness by the sages of India, as taught in the Hindu scriptures, the Upanishads. This volume is very abstruse, and beyond comprehension to most readers. Although Mrs. Eddy made little mention of Hinduism in any of her writings, she did deny any connection or similarity between Christian Science and Theosophy or Spiritualism.[9] She refuted a charge of being pantheistic by writing that Christian Science "finds spirit neither in matter nor in the modes of mortal mind."[10] The denials indicated that questions were being asked concerning the apparent similarity between Christian Science and oriental mysticism. Charles Samuel Bra-

9. Mary Baker Eddy, *No and Yes* (Boston: Allison V. Stewart, for the trustees under the will of Mary Baker Eddy, 1910), p. 13.
10. Ibid., p. 15.

den, in his volume *These Also Believe,* sums it up by suggesting that:

> The closest approximation to the thought of Mrs. Eddy is to be found in the Hindu concept of the one Real, and the illusory character of all else. So, also, her fundamental denial of the reality of evil and suffering is an almost exact restatement of one phase of Hindu thought.[11]

THE DOCTRINE OF JESUS CHRIST

A. In Christian Science, Jesus and the Christ are not the same. "The advent of Jesus of Nazareth marked the first century of the Christian era, but the Christ is without beginning or end of days" (SH 333:16-18). Jesus is simply the "human man" (SH 473:15) who "demonstrated Christ" (SH 332:19), being "the son of a virgin" (SH 332:23). Christ, on the other hand, is "the ideal Truth" (SH 473: 10), the "divine idea" (SH 473:16), "the spiritual or true idea of God" (SH 347:14-15), the "divine message from God to men . . . incorporeal, spiritual,—yea, the divine image and likeness, . . . the Way, the Truth, and the Life" (SH 332:10-14), "without beginning of years or end of days," (SH 333:18), the "reflection of God" (SH 333:21).

The incongruity of this entire teaching is startling and puzzling when we recall that it is taught that neither birth nor death is real. "Can there be any birth or death for man, the spiritual image and likeness of God?" (SH 206:25-26).

In a lengthy and much qualified explanation of the difference between Jesus and the Christ, Mrs. Eddy wrote: "The invisible Christ was imperceptible to the so-called personal sense, whereas Jesus appeared as a bodily existence. This dual personality . . . continued until the Master's ascension, when the human, material concept, or Jesus, disappeared, while the spiritual self, or Christ, continues

---

11. Charles Samuel Braden, *These Also Believe* (New York: Macmillan, 1949), p. 189.

to exist in the eternal order of divine Science, taking away the sins of the world, as the Christ has always done, even before the human Jesus was incarnate to mortal eyes" (SH 334:10-20).

It is not explained how there could be a corporeal Jesus, a "human, material concept," when nothing corporeal or material really exists. Perhaps explanation is withheld as impossible of understanding by those not enlightened, whose minds are "befogged in error." It should be noted that the Christ is eternal, is inseparable from the divine Principle, and is called the "divine idea." The man Jesus was simply the temporary vehicle through which the Christ was demonstrated. The corporeal Jesus was not "one with the Father, but . . . the spiritual idea, Christ, dwells forever in the bosom of the Father" (SH 334:3-5).

B. The virgin birth is intimated in the statement that "Jesus was the son of a virgin" (SH 332:23). But the commonly held belief that God the Son thus became incarnate through the body of the virgin could not be tenable to this strange system which denies the reality of any matter. "Mary's conception of him was spiritual" (SH 332:26-27). She "conceived this idea of God, and gave to her ideal the name of Jesus—that is, Joshua, or Saviour" (SH 29:17-18). Jesus was "the offspring of Mary's self-conscious communion with God" (SH 29:32—30:1).

C. The glossary of *Science and Health* defines *death* as "an illusion, the lie of life in matter, the unreal and untrue; the opposite of life" (SH 584:9-10). Reference is made to the illusion of the disciples of Jesus, who believed him to be dead "while he was hidden in the sepulchre, whereas he was alive" (SH 44:28-29). Bodily resurrection is dismissed with the definition that resurrection is "spiritualization of thought; a new and higher idea of immortality, or spiritual existence; material belief yielding to spiritual understanding" (SH 593:9-11).

Mrs. Eddy acknowledged that Christ Jesus was the "Way-shower" (SH 497:15) and that "man is saved through Christ, through Truth, Life, and Love, as demonstrated by the Galilean prophet" (SH 497:16-18). His "crucifixion and resurrection served to uplift faith to understanding eternal Life" (SH 497:20-21). He did not die, however, although his disciples believed him to be dead. He was alive in the tomb, demonstrating the power of "Spirit" (SH 44:31) to overrule material sense. It was thus that he "fully and finally demonstrated divine Science" (SH 45:6-7).

It naturally follows that there was no bodily resurrection. The illusory concept is carried through, however, in that "our Master reappeared to his students," that is, "to their apprehension he rose from the grave,—on the third day of his ascending thought [?]" (SH 509:4-7). To add to the confusion, it is also stated that he showed himself to his disciples to prove to their "physical senses that his body was not changed" (SH 46:14-15). It was for this purpose that he caused Thomas to "examine the nail-prints and the spear-wound" (SH 46:18-19). "In his final demonstration, called the ascension, which closed the earthly record of Jesus, he rose above the physical knowledge of his disciples, and the material sense saw him no more" (SH 46:26-29).

It is impossible to equate Christian Science with biblical Christianity in reference to Jesus Christ, His birth, His life, His death, His person, the atonement, His resurrection, and His ascension. There is not a single facet of His person and work that has not been distorted or denied.

THE DOCTRINE OF MAN

What is man? This question is treated at considerable length in the "Recapitulation" chapter of *Science and Health*. The answer begins:

Man is not matter; he is not made up of brain, blood, bones, and other material elements. . . . Man is made in the image and likeness of God. . . . Man is spiritual and perfect. . . . Man is idea, the image, of Love; he is not physique. He is the compound idea of God, including all right ideas; the generic term for all that reflects God's image and likeness; . . . man is the reflection of God, or Mind, and therefore is eternal [SH 475:6-18].

In view of this, it is declared that "man is incapable of sin, sickness, and death. The real man cannot depart from holiness, nor can God . . . engender the capacity or freedom to sin" (SH 475:28-31).

The follower of Mrs. Eddy who appears to be ill is exhorted never to say "I am sick." This is tantamount to saying that God is sick. He is to remind himself that he reflects God. "God is not sick. Therefore I am not sick." The practitioner emphasizes, "Man is the idea of God. The real *you* is that spiritual man. Know the truth! Know the truth! The truth will make you free." Free, that is, from the illusion of sin, sickness, and death.

Through all of this, there is a subtle indication that in dealing with "man," Mrs. Eddy was not writing about "men," or personal individual beings. She suddenly changes to the subject of "mortal beings," who are the "children of the wicked one, . . . which declares that man begins in dust or as a material embryo" (SH 476:2-4). Since the real man and God are inseparable, man is not mortal. It is not clear as to the relationship between man and mortals, for mortals are " 'conceived in sin and brought forth in iniquity' " (SH 476:16-17). This is strange language to one who denies both sin and iniquity. However, "mortals" are exhorted "earnestly [to] seek the spiritual status of man, which is outside of all material selfhood" (SH 476:21-22). This exhortation is embodied in the repeated command,

"Know the truth." The truth is that God is All-in-all, and that "you" are inseparable from God.

It would appear that part of the illusion of mortal mind lies in the concept of the individual soul. Any such idea of individuality is in opposition to the oft-repeated statement that God is All-in-all. The suggestion that "immortal" is contained in separate "mortals" would lead to the unthinkable conclusion that "Soul, or Spirit, is subdivided into spirits, or souls—alias gods."[12] What, therefore, is man? He is the "image and likeness of God, coexistent and coeternal with him . . . forever individual; . . . but what this individuality is, remains to be learned."[13] The only certainty is that the perfect man is not subject to birth or death. "Harmonious and immortal man has existed for ever, and is always beyond and above the mortal illusion of any life, . . . as existent in matter" (SH 302:15-18).

THE DOCTRINE OF SALVATION

There is no doctrine of salvation within Christian Science, as the term *salvation* is commonly understood. In view of what has been written above, the question might be asked, Who is to be saved from what? Mrs. Eddy gave this definition of salvation: "Life, Truth, and Love understood and demonstrated as supreme over all; sin, sickness, and death destroyed" (SH 593:20-22). The basic fact concerning sin is that unrealities seem real to the erring belief of mortal minds. "Christ came to destroy the belief of sin" (SH 473:6-7).

But it is elsewhere declared that sin brings suffering, and that "they who sin must suffer" (SH 37:2-3). So the idea persists that the coming of Christ was somehow related to the illusion of sin. The *Christ* did make a spiritual offering. But it is emphasized that the "*material* blood of

12. Eddy, *No and Yes*, p. 26.
13. Ibid., p. 25.

Jesus was no more efficacious to cleanse from sin when it was shed upon 'the accursed tree,' than when it was flowing in his veins as he went daily about his Father's business" (SH 25:6-8, italics added).

The enigmas are obvious. If matter is nonexistent, and suffering and death are unreal, how could Jesus Christ have suffered on the cross? If sin, disease, and death are all unreal, how could it be that "every pang of repentance and suffering . . . will help us to understand Jesus' atonement for sin and aid its efficacy" (SH 19:17-19).

The great work of Jesus, however, was to teach "the way of Life by demonstration" (SH 25:13). He was essentially the Way-shower, and the efficacy of the crucifixion lay in the "practical affection and goodness it demonstrated for mankind" (SH 24:27-28). This is summed up in the fourth of the religious tenets of Christian Science.

> We acknowledge Jesus' atonement as the evidence of divine, efficacious Love, unfolding man's unity with God through Jesus Christ the Way-shower; and we acknowledge that man is saved through Christ, through Truth, Life, and Love as demonstrated by the Galilean Prophet in healing the sick and overcoming sin and death [SH 497:13-19].

THE DOCTRINE OF THE FUTURE

Eschatology has little or no place in Christian Science. Heaven and hell are not places. Heaven is "harmony; the reign of Spirit; . . . the atmosphere of Soul" (SH 587:25-27). Hell is "mortal belief; error, lust; . . . suffering and self-destruction, self-imposed agony; effects of sin" (SH 588:1-3). When the apostle cried, "Now is the accepted time" (2 Cor. 6:2), he meant, "not that now men must prepare for a future-world salvation, or safety, but that now is the time in which to experience that salvation in spirit and in life" (SH 39:18-22). This means that "now is the time for so-called material pains and material pleasures to pass away, for both are unreal, because impossible in Science" (SH 39:22-24).

The declaration that man is "coexistent and coeternal with God" strongly implies preexistence. Mrs. Eddy reasoned that if man did not exist before the material organization began, he could not exist after the body disintegrated. "If we live after death and are immortal, we must have lived before birth" (SH 429:21-23). The actuality of death is not admitted, however. It is only "another phase of the dream that existence can be material" (SH 427:13-14). The body cannot die, because matter has no life to surrender" (SH 426:30-31).

The possibility of reincarnation is denied by Christian Science. But the suggestion of some sort of transmigration is undeniable in the statement that "mortal belief dies to live again in renewed forms, only to go out at last forever" (SH 556:10-12). Here is another statement that is difficult to comprehend. "Mortals waken from the dream of death with bodies unseen by those who think they bury the body" (SH 429:17).

The need for cleansing, or for some kind of purification, is indicated in that "mortals need not fancy that belief in the experience of death will awaken them to glorified being" (SH 291:9-11).

> If the change called *death* destroyed the belief in sin, sickness, and death, happiness would be won at the moment of dissolution, and be forever permanent; but this is not so. Perfection is gained only by perfection. They who are unrighteous shall be unrighteous still, until in divine Science Christ, Truth, removes all ignorance and sin [SH 290:16-22].

Progression and probation are necessary, and "universal salvation . . . is unattainable without them" (SH 291:12-

13). To complete the scheme and deal with the possibility of regression rather than progression, Mrs. Eddy wrote in another place, "If man should not progress after death, but should remain in error, he would be inevitably self-annihilated."[14]

Hindu philosophy based on monism, with its teaching of truth-realization, absorption into the Infinite, and freedom from the bondage of illusion and ignorance, seems to have found a revival under a new name, Christian Science.

14. Eddy, *Miscellaneous Writings*, p. 2.

8

Seventh-Day Adventism

THE TITLE *Seventh-Day Adventism* includes the two emphases which led to the founding of the organization. First, the seventh day, Saturday, is to be kept for rest and worship. Second, the second coming of Christ is one of the cardinal doctrines of the faith.

Prominent in the beginning history of the movement was William Miller, a Baptist preacher. His study of the Bible led him to the conclusion that Christ would return to earth between March 21, 1843, and March 21, 1844. This was not an unusual emphasis in those days, as many were positively expecting the return of the Lord. The passing of the set dates did not eliminate the hope. During the same period there were those known as Seventh-Day Baptists. They worshiped on Saturday rather than on Sunday. The two emphases became associated in one group and Seventh-Day Adventism came into being. The official organization was founded in 1863, largely through the efforts and abilities of Mrs. Ellen G. White. She was recognized as a prophetess uniquely guided by the Holy Spirit.

This group is noted for its evangelistic and missionary outreach, and claims to have work in 190 countries with a worldwide membership of 3,065,837. Contributions during 1977 totaled $474,846,241. They have no formal creed or statement of belief. For this reason, statements have been made concerning Seventh-Day Adventism which have not been in accord with the consensus of accepted doctrine.

Seventh-Day Adventists Answer Questions on Doctrine, published in 1957, is an authoritative statement of the beliefs of this group and was the outcome of a need and desire for clearer understanding of the teaching and objectives of the group.

> In this official statement Adventists affirm without equivocation that they stand with historic evangelical Christianity on these doctrines: The Trinity; the pre-existence and deity of Christ, His Virgin birth and sinless life, His vicarious, atoning death, His bodily resurrection and ascension and priestly ministry and mediation, His premillennial return; the deity and personality of the Holy Spirit; the depravity of man; salvation through Christ by grace alone, through faith in His blood; the entrance upon new life through regeneration; justification by faith; sanctification through the Spirit.[1]

Doctrines maintained by Seventh-Day Adventists which are taught by some other Christian groups include conditional immortality (soul sleep), annihilation of the wicked dead, and the keeping of the seventh day as the Sabbath. Of the doctrines that are unique and distinctive with Seventh-Day Adventists, there are three that are at best controversial: the emphasis upon the gift of the spirit of prophecy manifested in Ellen G. White, the entrance of Christ into the heavenly sanctuary, and investigative judgment. These teachings have raised questions in the minds of many evangelicals as to the orthodoxy of the movement.

Sources of Authority

"The Holy Scriptures of the Old and New Testaments were given by inspiration of God, contain an all-sufficient

1. J. Oswald Sanders, *Cults and Isms* (Grand Rapids: Zondervan, 1962), p. 126.

revelation of His will to men, and are the only unerring rule of faith and practice."[2]

In spite of this clear statement, doubts arise concerning the place given to the writing of Mrs. White. Her name is constantly inserted in Seventh-Day Adventist distinctives as the one upon whom the spirit of prophecy, or the prophetic gift, was manifested. Her vision of Christ entering the heavenly sanctuary in 1844 is one of the prime reasons for the existence of the movement. Her writings are "slavishly and exclusively" recognized, in the opinion of Dr. Wilbur M. Smith.[3] The gift of prophecy was uniquely hers, and her writings are classified as "inspired counsel and instruction."[4]

THE DOCTRINE OF THE ATONEMENT—HEAVENLY SANCTUARY AND INVESTIGATIVE JUDGMENT

We take our stand without qualification on the gospel platform that the death of Jesus Christ provides the *sole* propitiation for our sins, (I John 2:2; 4:10); that there is salvation through no other means or medium, and no other name by which we may be saved (Acts 4:12); and that the shed blood of Jesus Christ *alone* brings remission for our sins (Mt. 26:28). That is foundational.[5]

The claim to orthodoxy with regard to this central doctrine of the Christian faith is greatly minimized by the unique teaching concerning the heavenly sanctuary and investigative judgment. The concept of the entrance of Christ into the heavenly sanctuary in 1844 was based primarily on a vision seen by Hiram Edson in 1844 and confirmed to Mrs. White in 1845. Edson's vision took place following the great disappointment, when Christ failed

2. *Seventh-Day Adventists Answer Questions on Doctrine* (Washington, D.C.: Review and Herald, 1957), p. 11 (hereafter cited as *Questions*).
3. In Walter R. Martin, *The Truth About Seventh-Day Adventism* (Grand Rapids: Zondervan, 1960), p. 96.
4. *Questions*, p. 92.
5. Ibid., p. 396.

to appear on October 22, 1844. He saw "that instead of our High Priest coming out of the Most Holy of the heavenly sanctuary to come to this earth on the tenth day of the seventh month, at the end of the 2300 days, He for the first time entered on that day the second apartment of that sanctuary."[6] Adventists interpret the 2,300 days (Dan. 8:14) to mean 2,300 years, reckoning a day for a year, as in Ezekiel 4:6 or Numbers 14:34. They believe that the "going forth of the commandment to restore and to build Jerusalem" (Dan. 9:25; Ezra 7:11-26) marked the date from which the 2,300 years were to be computed. The year in which authorization was given to Ezra to restore Jerusalem was 457 B.C. Twenty-three hundred years from 457 B.C. reaches to A.D. 1844. "Seventh-day Adventists believe, therefore, that some important event in God's plan was scheduled to start in the year 1844—in the symbolic language of the prophecy, 'the sanctuary [shall] be cleansed.' "[7] This is explained from the typology of the ancient Jewish sanctuary.

The sanctuary in the wilderness and in the temple are believed to be the object lessons of God's plan of redemption. Two phases of ministry were related to the sanctuary. One was performed in the outer court every day of the year. This was the work of reconciliation by which, explain the Adventists, the sin was transferred from the sinner to the victim, and to the priest. The record of the sin remained in the sanctuary as the sacrificial blood was sprinkled. The second phase was that of the Day of Atonement, performed only once each year. On that day "when the blood of the goat was sprinkled upon all that furniture of the sanctuary as well as upon the altar of burnt offering, the accumulated record of the sins of the year were re-

6. In Anthony A. Hoekema, *The Four Major Cults* (Grand Rapids: Eerdmans, 1963), p. 92.
7. *Questions,* p. 429.

moved."[8] In other words, confessed sins were expunged, or blotted out.

Adventists believe, therefore, that on the cross of Calvary an all-sufficient sacrifice has been provided; and that from the time of Christ's ascension until 1844 He had been carrying on the work of "forgiveness," comparable to that of the priests in their daily ministry. Since October 22, 1844, His work has been comparable to that of the high priest on the Day of Atonement. This is called investigative judgment, and will culminate in the complete blotting out of the sins of all true believers.

Investigative judgment deals largely with the book of life (Rev. 20:15), which is the register of all professed believers, beginning with those who first lived upon the earth. The record of each will be scrutinized by the Lord Jesus Christ. Some will be found to have sins remaining upon the record, unrepented of and unforgiven. Their names will be blotted out of the book, in the Adventist interpretation of Exodus 32:33 with Revelation 3:5. This is understood to indicate that "the acceptance of Christ at conversion does not seal a person's destiny. . . . Nor can it be said that a man's record is closed when he comes to the end of his days. He is responsible for his influence during life, and is just as surely responsible for his evil influence after he is dead."[9] In this light the book of life is examined. Those who have truly repented of all sin, and have claimed the blood, and have continued their allegiance throughout life, will be judged worthy to have a part in the first resurrection of life. It must be noted, however, that sins confessed and forgiven remain on the record until life is complete, because "subsequent deeds and attitudes may affect the final decision."[10] In other words,

8. Ibid., p. 432.
9. Ibid., p. 420.
10. Ibid., p. 441.

forgiveness may be canceled. In the ultimate sense, one's salvation depends upon his conversion and upon his maintenance of acceptable character.

The final blotting out of sins takes place when "Christ . . . removes the sins of His people from the heavenly sanctuary," and places them upon Satan, "who, in the execution of the judgment, must bear the final penalty."[11] Satan thus becomes the scapegoat of Leviticus 16:8. "Satan, bearing the guilt of all the sins which he has caused God's people to commit, will be for a thousand years confined to the earth . . . and he will at last suffer the full penalty of sin in the fires that shall destroy all the wicked."[12] While there is ambiguity in the language of Leviticus 16:8, this teaching concerning the scapegoat is not generally accepted by evangelical Christians. They believe that the goat which is sent away into the wilderness, nevermore to be seen or heard of, typifies the everlasting oblivion into which the sins of believers have been cast—to be remembered no more. The two goats represent two sides of the complete work of the Lord Jesus Christ on Calvary. To make Satan the scapegoat implies that he is in some degree our sin bearer. It is only fair to note that this implication is repudiated by the authorities who wrote *Seventh-Day Adventists Answer Questions on Doctrine*. "The thought [that Satan is in any sense or degree our sin bearer] is abhorrent to us, and appallingly sacrilegious."[13] "Satan makes no atonement for our sins. But Satan will ultimately have to bear the retributive punishment for his responsibility in the sins of all men, both righteous and wicked."[14]

11. Ellen G. White, *The Great Controversy*, p. 422. Quoted by Hoekema, p. 120.
12. White, *The Great Controversy*, pp. 485-86. Quoted by Hoekema, p. 120.
13. *Questions*, p. 400.
14. Ibid.

THE DOCTRINE OF THE SABBATH

Outwardly the best known and most obvious distinctive of Seventh-Day Adventists is the observance of Saturday as the Sabbath. The teaching is that the keeping of the fourth commandment is of particular significance. Mrs. White saw, in a vision, the Ten Comamndments in the ark. There was a halo of glory around the Sabbath commandment. Therefore, the keeping of the seventh day as the Sabbath is regarded as a "test of . . . loyalty to Christ as Creator and Redeemer."[15] The oft-repeated charge that failure to observe the Sabbath is the "mark of the Beast" has been consistently repudiated by Seventh-Day Adventist authorities. Mrs. White declared, "Sunday keeping is not yet the mark of the beast. . . . The time will come when this day will be the test, but that test has not come yet."[16] The doctrinal book published in 1957 affirms, "Seventh-day Adventists do not rely upon their Sabbath keeping as a *means* of salvation or of winning merit before God."[17]

THE DOCTRINES OF CONDITIONAL IMMORTALITY AND OF THE ANNIHILATION OF THE WICKED DEAD

The doctrines of conditional immortality and of the annihilation of the wicked dead are not unique or distinctive with Seventh-Day Adventism. They are stated succinctly among the "Fundamental Beliefs of Seventh-day Adventists":

> 9. . . . "God only hath immortality" (I Tim. 6:16). Mortal man possesses a nature inherently sinful and dying. . . . Immortality is bestowed upon the righteous at the second coming of Christ, when the righteous dead are raised from the grave and the living righteous translated

15. Ibid., p. 153.
16. Ellen G. White, Manuscript 118, 1899. Quoted in Sanders, p. 131.
17. *Questions,* p. 153.

to meet the Lord. Then it is that those accounted faithful "put on immortality."

10. . . . The condition of man in death is one of unconsciousness. All men, good and evil alike, remain in the grave from death to the resurrection. . . .

11. . . . There shall be a resurrection both of the just and of the unjust. The resurrection of the just will take place at the second coming of Christ; the resurrection of the unjust will take place a thousand years later, at the close of the millennium.

12. . . . The finally impenitent, including Satan, the author of sin, will, by the fires of the last day, be reduced to a state of nonexistence, becoming as though they had not been, thus purging God's universe of sin and sinners.[18]

The Doctrine of Things to Come

The imminent second coming of Christ will involve judgment and total defeat of the world's rebellious sinners at Armageddon. While believers will be caught up, the unbelieving will be "left on the earth, dead, for the birds to consume."[19]

Satan will be confined to the earth during the millennial period. The earth will be a place of utter desolation, all the physical aspects of its surface having been destroyed. There Satan must "await amid this desolation the final disposition of the cases of all the unredeemed in the court above."[20]

At the close of this period, the wicked dead are raised. Satan is also released and marshals the wicked into a final attempt to overthrow the Kingdom of God. Then it is that the "entire human race meets face to face for the first and last time."[21] The great drama of the ages ends with Satan's final and irrevocable overthrow and utter extinc-

18. Ibid., pp. 13-14.
19. Ibid., p. 496.
20. Ibid., p. 500.
21. Ibid., p. 505.

tion. He and all that follow him will be totally annihilated when fire comes down out of heaven.

The close of the millennial period will bring in the beginning of the eternal, new earth-state. God will make all things new, and the earth will become forever the dwelling place of the saints of the Lord.

9

Other Current Movements

A CHARACTERISTIC OF THE PRESENT DAY is the resurgence of the old religions of the world. Hinduism and Buddhism are awakening to make inroads into Occidental society. Various organizations in the West are actively propagating the teaching of the Hindu philosophy called Vedanta and spreading various shades of Buddhist doctrine. Baha'ism arose from a Muslim background but is notably eclectic in its sympathetic attitude toward all major religions. Other new systems have been created from segments of the old which have been transplanted into Christian settings, using Christian terminology. Most of these tend to syncretism. That is, they combine biblical teaching with other beliefs and practices. They do not claim to be Christian, and they uniformly dispense with any form of dogmatism. Common among them is the concept that "as all rivers lead to the ocean, so all roads ultimately lead to eternal peace." The best thing, according to many, is to choose the way that suits best and to work hard at it.

Of the current systems with some influence, several are notably Hindu in their major beliefs. This has been noted concerning Christian Science, which seems to have provided the impetus for similar groups. These deny or doubt the personality of God and impugn the reality of matter, sin, sickness, and death. Christ is a principle which is in all men, although seen in perfection in Jesus. Salvation is attained by the realization of the oneness of the individual with the All-in-all. This is the At-one-ment! In most, re-incarnation is taught as the means by which all may have the opportunity to attain immortality as Jesus did.

THEOSOPHY

THE NAME *Theosophy* is compounded from two Greek words, and means "knowledge of God," or "God-knowledge," or "divine wisdom." It denotes an eclectic philosophic-religious system which was founded in 1875 in New York. Admittedly derived from Hinduism, it does not claim any new concepts but presumes to present truths which are common to all religions. These beliefs form "in their entirety, the Wisdom-Religion, or the Universal Religion, the source from which all separate religions spring, the trunk of the Tree of Life from which they all branch forth."[1] It is maintained that the essence of all true religion is

> the knowledge of the One, whom knowing, all else is known, the knowledge of Him, that is the supreme, the highest knowledge. That is Theosophy. That is the knowledge of God which is eternal life.[2]

No member of the Theosophical Society is asked to believe or to preach theosophical teachings. He may profess whatever religion he pleases, since there is essential truth in all.

THE DOCTRINE OF GOD

It is taught that God exists and that He is good. But it is the god of Hindu pantheism, or better, monism. Any thought of personality is untenable. Madame Blavatsky, first among the propagators of this revamped Hinduism, so declared: "We believe in a Universal Divine Principle, the

1. Annie Besant, *Theosophy* (London and Edinburgh: T. C. & E. C. Jack, Ltd., n.d.), p. 12.
2. Annie Besant, *Popular Lectures on Theosophy* (Chicago: Rajput Press, 1910), p. 4.

root of ALL, from which all proceeds, and within which all shall be absorbed at the end of the great cycle of Being."[3] This concept is amplified by Mrs. Besant, the other notable leader: "There is no grain of dust in which God's life is not immanent. . . . There is no other life than His; there is no other consciousness than His; there is no other Will than His. . . . There is only one life, one consciousness, and one power, and that is the life, consciousness and power of Ishvara (God), that are in all that He has emanated."[4] If one would know the hidden mystery, the divine Spirit, he is advised: "Find Him first in your own Self, and then you will see Him everywhere. . . . This is the Divine Wisdom, which we call Theosophy."[5]

The Doctrine of Jesus Christ

Theosophy teaches about the hierarchy of supernatural beings who come in descending scale from the Lord of the World. These include the Adepts, or Mahatmas (Great Souls). They are the ultimate in human evolution, perfected men who choose to be reincarnated for the good of humanity.

The Lord of all these becomes incarnate from time to time as the Divine Teacher. He enters the body of one who is worthy. Jesus Christ was the fifth of these up to the present and is the master to whom the Christian should turn. Of course, it is recognized that there are other divine teachers in other faiths, worthy of the same worship of their own followers.

The Doctrine of Man

Man is an exceedingly complex being. He is called a "divine Fragment," and his ultimate destiny is absorption

3. H. P. Blavatsky, *The Key to Theosophy* (1889; reprint ed., Covina, Calif.: Theosophical University Press, 1946), p. 63.
4. In Charles Samuel Braden, *These Also Believe* (New York: Macmillan, 1949), p. 244.
5. Besant, *Popular Lectures on Theosophy*, p. 5.

in the impersonal god. Actually, man is " 'God' and not *a* god."[6] The true man is an emanation from the Logos, a spark of the divine. The human soul, in essence, is not to be distinguished from the Universal Soul. Man is said to have one spirit, three souls, one life principle, and two bodies, the physical and the astral.

Man is immortal. Death is merely the passage from one stage of being into another.

The Doctrine of Salvation

Salvation is by the evolutionary passing of the soul into higher incarnations. Linked inseparably with this doctrine of reincarnation is the Hindu doctrine of Karma. This is the Law of Action and Re-action, expressed in the words, "As a man soweth, so also shall he reap." All good or evil committed produces fruit in this or in successive lives. The professed aim of life is an ordered progress through these incarnations until the ultimate goal of oneness with the divine is attained.

The individual can cooperate intelligently in his own evolution. "It is . . . part of this plan [the Divine scheme] for man's evolution that he himself should intelligently cooperate in it as soon as he has developed sufficient intelligence to grasp it."[7] There must be innate capacity plus earnest desire. Much time is necessary, plus self-sacrifice, abandonment of earthly ties and ambitions, and considerable self-discipline. The end is not easily reached. "As in the case of any other science, so in this science of the soul, full details are known only to those who devote their lives to its pursuit. The men who fully know—those who are called Adepts—have patiently developed within themselves the powers necessary for perfect observation."[8] "It has

6. Blavatsky, p. 67.
7. C. W. Leadbeater, *An Outline of Theosophy* (Chicago: Theosophical Book Concern, 1903), pp. 29-30.
8. Ibid., p. 9.

been proved," wrote Mrs. Besant, "and can ever be re-
proved, that thought, concentrating itself attentively on
any idea, builds that idea into the character of the thinker,
and a man may thus create in himself any desirable quality
by sustained and attentive thinking—meditation."[9]

The idea in mind is an ecstatic vision of the Ultimate,
of Unknowable, in which the distinction between the individual self and the Primal Being is obliterated. This is
Theosophy, or Divine Wisdom.

THE UNITY SCHOOL OF CHRISTIANITY

THE NAME *Unity School of Christianity* is aptly chosen,
and it embodies the central principle of the organization:
"Unity of the soul with God, unity of all life, unity of all
religions, unity of the spirit, soul, and body; unity of all men
in the heart of truth."[1] The only right to the inclusion of
the words *of Christianity* is that Unity carries on its activity
within the realm of nominal Christianity. The organization claims no membership, and its adherents are members
of churches throughout the country. It was at one time
reckoned by one authority that "more than one-third of
denominationally identified Christians in the United States
have read or are reading Unity material."[2]

There is no one source of authority other than the writings of the organization. It is maintained that "Truth" is
not static, but ever increasing. Unity strives to interpret
the Bible, but it does not claim either infallibility or final-
ity.

The concept of God is impersonal. God is "Principle,
Law, Being, Mind, Spirit, All Good, omnipotent, omnis-

---

9. Besant, *Theosophy*, pp. 56-57.
1. Marcus Bach, *They Have Found a Faith* (Indianapolis: Bobbs-
   Merrill, 1946), p. 223.
2. Russell P. Spittler, *Cults and Isms* (Grand Rapids: Baker, 1962), p.
   73.

cient, unchangeable, Creator, Father, Cause and Source of all that is."[3]

Unity's aim is to bring about the realization of the oneness, or unity, of the individual with God, with infinite, omnipotent Being. The founder, Charles Fillmore, wrote: "Drop from your minds the belief that God is in any way separated from you, that He occupies form or space outside of you, or that He can be manifested to your consciousness in any way except through your own soul."[4]

The Unity concept of Jesus Christ sounds like that of Theosophy. Like Gnosticism, Unity denies the complete and absolute deity of Jesus Christ. He was a perfected soul who attained creative power in a cosmic evolution previous to human history. Jesus and the Christ, however, are not the same. They are separate entities who occupied the same body for a time. Jesus was a man, as we are. Christ is the cosmic spirit of the universe, of which every man is a part. In order to "realize" this, Unity advocates the repetition of such statements as this:

> I am the Son of God, and the Spirit of the most High dwells in me;
> I am the Christ of God.
> He who hath seen me hath seen the Father.
> I and my Father are one.[5]

There is some ambiguity concerning evil, which at times seems to exist, and at times is denied existence. At any rate, sickness and disease are the result of inward conditions, conquerable by the ancient yogic method of concentration upon the fact that the individual soul is one with the Infinite.

3. Charles Samuel Braden, *These Also Believe* (New York: Macmillan, 1949), p. 157.
4. In Ibid.
5. Charles Fillmore, *The Science of Being and Christian Healing* (Kansas City, Mo.: Unity Tract Society, 1920), pp. 27-28.

Ultimate salvation is connected with the belief in re-incarnation, and is attained when the cycle of birth is broken and man comes to birth no more. As expressed in Unity's statement of faith, "We believe that the dissolution of spirit, soul, and body caused by death, is annulled by rebirth of the same spirit and soul in another body here on earth. We believe the repeated incarnations of man to be a merciful provision of our loving Father to the end that all may have opportunity to attain immortality through regeneration, as did Jesus."

THE "I AM" MOVEMENT

A CURSORY READING of *The "I AM" Decrees* reveals that there is little if anything new in this system. A central concept is that of the Ascended Masters who are the custodians of the "Eternal Inner Understanding" of the "I AM, the Great Creative Word." The Ascended Master, Saint Germain, is chief among thousands, and is the one through whom this teaching came to its founders.

The conception of God is pantheistic. "Life in all its activities everywhere manifest, is *God in Action,* and it is only through lack of understanding of applied thought and feeling that mankind is constantly interrupting" the pure flow of that Perfect Essence of Life, "I AM" is the Activity of "That Life."[1] "When you say and feel 'I AM,' you release the spring of Eternal, Everlasting Life, to flow on its way unmolested. In other words, you open wide the door to Its natural flow. . . . 'I AM' is the Full Activity of God."[2] The repetition of the words "I AM" is to bring the experiential realization that there is no other being besides oneself. "The student is admonished to look always, and never forget it, to his own God Self, which is the Creator of his in

1. Godfré Ray King, *The "I AM" Discourses* (Chicago: St. Germain Press, 1936), p. 2.
2. Ibid., pp. 2-3.

dividualization."[3] "When the student can once understand that the Ascended Host of Masters are but the more advanced consciousness of himself, then he will begin to feel the unquestionable possibilities within his grasp. Whether he speaks to the Godhead direct, to one of the Ascended Masters of Light or to his own God Self, in reality it makes no difference, for all are One. Until one does reach this state of consciousness, it does make a difference, for the individual is almost certain to feel a division of the One Self, which is not possible to be made, except in the ignorance of the outer activity of the mind."[4] For this reason there is no sickness, for divinity cannot be sick.

Man is on the cosmic wheel of existence, and can only escape by the comprehension of the truth as given. Any one who dies without grasping the truth of the Law of Life must return in another body and try again to secure the victory.

BAHA'ISM

BAHA'ISM DIFFERS from all other cults discussed in that its roots are in Islam. It is, however, quite un-Islamic in its lack of positive dogma and in its eclecticism. Baha'ism claims to be the fulfillment of past revelations of the world's major religions. It "upholds the unity of God, recognizes the unity of His Prophets, and inculcates the principle of the oneness and wholeness of the entire human race."[1]

The first recognized founder was known as The Bab, or "Gate," and lived in Persia. In 1844 he proclaimed himself the messenger whose coming had been foretold by Muhammad. His successor was known as Baha'u'llah, "The Glory of God." He declared, "plainly and repeatedly, that he was the long-expected educator and teacher of all peo-

3. Ibid., p. 27.
4. Ibid., p. 28.
1. Shoghi Effendi, *The Faith of Baha'u'llah* (Wilmette, Ill.: Baha'i Publishing Trust, 1959), pp. 7-8.

ples, the channel of a wondrous Grace that would tran-
scend all previous outpourings, in which all previous forms
of religion would be merged, as rivers merge in the ocean."[2]
He was to bring about the inauguration of the glorious age
of peace on earth foretold by prophets of old. It would be
characterized by unity of mankind, religions, races, nations; equality of men and women; unification of languages; one international tribunal for judgment of all. The
Baha'i World Faith is named after Baha'u'llah. With him
it was claimed, "the Prophetic Cycle hath verily ended.
The Eternal Truth is now come."[3]

It is singular that out of the dogmatism of inflexible
Islam should come a religion which teaches that all religions are one. The concept of deity is at times Islamic,
and at other times it savors of pantheism. No member of
the human family is bad, or evil. "Sin" is defined as the absence of good in the life of the faithful. Therefore atonement is unnecessary. "Education will free men from all im-
perfections."[4] The founders of all major religions were
messengers of God by whom the evolution of human society has progressed. Baha'u'llah is the voice of God for
this age. In him the culmination has been reached.

SWEDENBORGIANISM—THE CHURCH OF
THE NEW JERUSALEM

CALLED "THE NEW CHURCH" BY ITS MEMBERS, Swedenborgianism, or The Church of the New Jerusalem, takes
its unique teachings from the religious writings of Emanuel Swedenborg (1688-1772). He was a noted scientist
and philosopher who devoted the last thirty years of his
life to "a comprehensive restatement of the Christian message." This study followed a "profound religious experi-

---

2. J. E. Esslemont, *Baha'u'llah and the New Era* (Wilmette, Ill.:
   Baha'i Publishing Committee, 1948), p. 7.
3. *Baha'i World Faith: Selected Writings of Baha'u'llah and Abdu'l
   Baha* (Wilmette, Ill.: Baha'i Publishing Trust, 1956), title page.
4. Ibid., p. 319.

ence which was accompanied by an opening of his consciousness into the world of spirit."[1] His Latin volumes of doctrinal and biblical interpretation and other-world disclosures number more than thirty.

The Church of the New Jerusalem was organized in London in 1787. It claims to be a Protestant church, founded upon the Bible, with its central teaching about "the Lord God." However, a better evaluation is found in the statement that "we are a teaching church, seeking to make Christian theology understood and reasonable to the enquiring mind."[2] In fundamental doctrines, Swedenborgianism is utterly at odds with orthodox Christianity. Sufficient to prove this are these statements from Swedenborg's *True Christian Religion:*

> The passion of the cross was the last temptation which the Lord, as the greatest Prophet, endured; also it was a means of glorifying His Human, that is, of uniting it with the Divine of the Father; but it was not redemption.[3]
>
> The belief that the passion of the cross was redemption itself is a fundamental error of the church; and this error, together with the error respecting three Divine Persons from eternity, has perverted the whole church so that nothing spiritual is left in it.[4]

The "final judgment" took place in 1757, at which time the "new dispensation" began. Since then the Lord has been engaged in "performing a redemption" which pertains to the subjugation of the hells and establishment of order in the heavens. This is in preparation for a new spiritual church.

In rejecting the orthodox doctrine of the Trinity, Swe-

1. Explanatory card issued by Church of the Holy City, Washington, D.C.
2. Bulletin of the Church of the Holy City, Washington, D.C.
3. Emanuel Swedenborg, *True Christian Religion* (Boston and New York: Houghton Mifflin, 1949), 1:175.
4. Ibid.

denborg taught that God exists in His one person in three ways:

God in the depths of His Being is the Father;
God knowable and known is the Son;
God actively and always engaged in imparting of Himself is the Holy Spirit.

Christ is believed to have inherited evil from his mother. But "God has revealed Himself most completely in the person of Jesus Christ who overcame the limitations of His human nature until He became one with God."[5]

The efficacy of the cross having been set aside, the bodily resurrection is denied. It is declared that "the Lord Jesus Christ appeared to the spiritually alert senses of the disciples as the very same beloved Lord and Master whom they thought had 'died' on the cross."[6] The regeneration mentioned in the third chapter of John is a spiritual matter, and in that sense we are reborn every time a new affection possesses us. Man lives on earth only once. This one existence determines character, and the character established here in life is maintained in the hereafter. At death, the person enters a "world of spirits," which is a state between heaven and hell. There two ways of life are presented to every person. The choice is a free one, for "our Lord said, 'I judge no man.'" Actually the judgment seat is in our own hearts, for we judge ourselves by the choices we make. In the world of spirits the selfish and vile man may change, but unfortunately we tend to react on the basis of past reactions. The good man seeks more of what is good and true; the sinner finds boon companions. And so we pass on to the Further Life. Spiritual failures go to the environment suited to their natures, in bondage to insatiable desires. "All-consuming passions con-

5. Bulletin of the Church of the Holy City, Washington, D.C.
6. *Life Further On* (Philadelphia: American New-Church Tract and Publishing Society, n.d.), p. 28.

tinue to burn, and to leave him frustrated. That is hell."[7] Heaven is the place where the fundamentally honest man finds his like. It is a real world, with cities, churches, schools, homes, and gardens; and it is filled with men and women who have cultivated the fine things of life, each doing what he is most interested in doing and can do best. It is a society of redeemed men and women—a human achievement.

ROSICRUCIANISM (THE ROSE CROSS)

THE ORDER OF ROSICRUCIANS was founded in 1313 by Chris Rosenkreuz. Its adherents see in the cross a symbol of "the life currents vitalizing the bodies of plants, animals, and man." The founder felt that his mission was to prepare a new phase of the Christian religion for the coming age (in which we now live) in order to keep pace with the normal progress in evolution. It is claimed that the philosophy is entirely Christian, "striving to lead to Christ those who cannot find Him by faith alone."[1] It seeks to foster the acceptance of Christian doctrines through the medium of esoteric knowledge. This knowledge is that which has been acquired from the ancients of Egypt, India, Tibet, Mexico, and other places.

The basic textbook is the *Rosicrucian Cosmo-Conception*, by Max Heindel. It is known as the Western Wisdom, given to the author by the elder Brothers of the Rose Cross. *Cosmo-Conception* "gives the most logical explanation of the universe and man's part in it from the viewpoint of evolution ever issued to the general public. The earlier ages vaguely referred to in Genesis are fully elucidated, showing how man started as a spark of the Divine Flame of God, and after aeons of preparation reached his present state, and will finally attain the perfection of superman."[2]

7. Ibid., p. 25.
1. *The Rosicrucian Interpretation of Christianity* (Oceanside, Calif.: Rosicrucian Fellowship, n.d.), p. 1.
2. Advertisement of Rosicrucian Fellowship, Oceanside, Calif.

There are currently two active organizations with the same teaching: The Rosicrucian Fellowship, in Oceanside, California, and the Ancient Mystical Order Rosae Crucis, known as AMORC, with headquarters in San Jose, California. The latter organization emphasizes that the Rosicrucians are *not* a religious organization, but "a non-sectarian fraternity devoted to the investigation and study of the higher principles of life as found expressed in man and nature."[3] It is interesting to note that the claimed connection with Egypt came through the acceptance of some of the fundamental teachings of the Gnostics and the Pythagorians. AMORC is strictly secret, spiritual, and free from dogma so that members of all religions may become acolytes. It is not a separate religion but fundamentally religious, teaching the immortality of the soul and the fatherhood of God.

The motto is "Try." One is saved not by another's intervention or substitution but by overcoming all evil. Everyone possesses an incorruptible seed, a divine spark, a Christos, which must be awakened and brought into consciousness. Christ is not the only begotten Son of God. He returns to earth every year, and offers a sacrifice. All will attain perfection by the normal process of reincarnation, although some will progress faster than others. The Law of Sowing and Reaping, the Hindu Karma, is operative in every life.

The centers of the orders carry on various activities. There are studies in philosophy, astrology, healing, printing, and Bible study. In certain areas the teaching is similar to that of Theosophy. There are the Seven Worlds, separated not by space or distance but by rate of vibrations. There are Invisible Helpers, who work on the spiritual planes to bring healing by raising the vibrations of the sick to higher levels. The appeal of Rosicrucianism is largely through its accent on the occult and the mysterious.

3. Letterhead of International Supreme Temple, San Jose, Calif.

Bibliography

GENERAL

Bach, Marcus. *They Have Found a Faith*. Indianapolis: Bobbs-Merrill, 1946.

Braden, Charles Samuel. *These Also Believe*. New York: Macmillan, 1949.

Ferm, Virgilius, ed. *Religion in the Twentieth Century*. New York: Philosophical Library, 1948.

Gerstner, John H. *The Theology of the Major Sects*. Grand Rapids: Baker, 1960.

Hoekema, Anthony A. *The Four Major Cults*. Grand Rapids: Eerdmans, 1963.

Lewis, Gordon R. *Confronting the Cults*. Nutley, N.J.: Presby. & Ref., 1966.

Sanders, J. Oswald. *Cults and Isms*. Grand Rapids: Zondervan, 1962.

Spittler, Russell P. *Cults and Isms*. Grand Rapids: Baker, 1962.

MORMONISM

The Book of Mormon. Salt Lake City: The Church of Jesus Christ of Latter-day Saints.

Doctrine and Covenants. Salt Lake City: The Church of Jesus Christ of Latter-day Saints.

Fraser, Gordon H. *Is Mormonism Christian?* Rev. ed. Chicago: Moody, 1977.

McConkie, Bruce R. *Mormon Doctrine*. Salt Lake City: Bookcraft, 1966.

Morgan, John. *The Plan of Salvation*. Salt Lake City: Deseret (pamphlet).

The Pearl of Great Price. Salt Lake City: The Church of Jesus Christ of Latter-day Saints.

Peterson, Mark E. *Which Church Is Right?* Salt Lake City: Deseret, n.d. (pamphlet).

Smith, Elbert A. *Differences That Persist.* Independence, Mo.: Herald Publishing House (publishing house of The Reorganized Church of Jesus Christ of Latter Day Saints).

Smith, Joseph F. *Gospel Doctrine.* Salt Lake City: Deseret, 1963.

Smith, Joseph Fielding. *Teachings of the Prophet Joseph Smith.* Salt Lake City: Deseret, 1958. Excerpts from sermons and writings of Joseph Smith.

Talmage, James E. *A Study of the Articles of Faith.* Salt Lake City: The Church of Jesus Christ of Latter-day Saints, 1961.

Tanner, Jerald, and Tanner, Sandra. *The Changing World of Mormonism.* Chicago: Moody, 1979.

Uniform System for Teaching Investigators. Salt Lake City: Deseret. Published for use only by Mormon missionaries.

Young, Brigham. *Journal of Discourses.* Liverpool, 1854-75.

JEHOVAH'S WITNESSES

Let God Be True. Brooklyn: Watchtower Bible and Tract Society, 1952.

Make Sure of All Things. Brooklyn: Watchtower Bible and Tract Society, 1953.

New Heavens and a New Earth. Brooklyn: Watchtower Bible and Tract Society, 1953.

New World Translation of the Holy Scriptures. Brooklyn: Watchtower Bible and Tract Society, 1961.

Studies in the Scriptures. 7 vols. Allegheny, Pa.: Watchtower Bible and Tract Society.

The Word—Who is He? Brooklyn: Watchtower Bible and Tract Society.

UNIFICATION CHURCH

Moon, Sun Myung. *Christianity in Crisis.* Washington, D.C.: Holy Spirit Association for the Unification of World Christianity, 1974.

———. *The Divine Principle*. Washington, D.C.: Holy Spirit Association for the Unification of World Christianity, 1973.

Sontag, Frederick. *Sun Myung Moon*. Nashville: Abingdon, 1977.

Yamamoto, J. Isamu. *The Puppet Master*. Downers Grove, Ill.: InterVarsity, 1977.

WORLDWIDE CHURCH OF GOD

Armstrong, Herbert W. *All About Water Baptism*. Pasadena, Calif.: Ambassador College Press, 1954.

———. *Does God Heal Today?* Pasadena, Calif.: Ambassador College Press, 1952.

———. *Lazarus and the Rich Man*. Pasadena, Calif.: Radio Church of God, 1953.

———. *Predestination—Does the Bible Teach It?* Pasadena, Calif.: Radio Church of God, 1957.

———. *The United States and the British Commonwealth in Prophecy*. Pasadena, Calif.: Ambassador College Press, 1954.

———. *Which Day Is the Sabbath of the New Testament?* Pasadena, Calif.: Ambassador College Press, 1952.

Benware, Paul N. *Ambassadors of Armstrongism*. Nutley, N.J.: Presby. & Ref., 1975.

Hopkins, Joseph. *The Armstrong Empire*. Grand Rapids: Eerdmans, 1974.

THE WAY INTERNATIONAL

Whiteside, Elena S. *The Way: Living in Love*. New Knoxville, Ohio: American Christian Press, 1972.

Wierwille, Victor Paul. *The Bible Tells Me So*. Studies in Abundant Living, vol. 1. New Knoxville, Ohio: American Christian Press, 1971.

———. *Jesus Christ Is Not God*. New Knoxville, Ohio: American Christian Press, 1975.

———. *The New, Dynamic Church*. Studies in Abundant Living, vol. 2. New Knoxville, Ohio: American Christian Press, 1971.

———. *The Word's Way*. Studies in Abundant Living, vol. 3. New Knoxville, Ohio: American Christian Press, 1971.

Williams, J. L. *Victor Paul Wierwille and the Way International*. Chicago: Moody, 1979.

EASTERN MYSTICISM

Braden, Charles Samuel. *The Scriptures of Mankind: An Introduction*. New York: Macmillan, 1952.

Cameron, Charles, ed. *Who is Guru Maharaj Ji?* New York: Bantam, 1973.

Isherwood, Christopher, ed. *Vedanta for Modern Man*. New York: Collier, 1962.

Noss, John B. *Man's Religions*. New York: Macmillan, 1956.

Prabhavananda Swami, and Isherwood, Christopher, trans. *Bhagavad-Gita: Song of God*. New York: Mentor Classic, 1951.

Yogi, Maharishi Mahesh. *Meditations of Maharishi Mahesh Yogi*. New York: Bantam, 1973.

CHRISTIAN SCIENCE

Dakin, Edwin F. *Mrs. Eddy, the Biography of a Virginal Mind*. New York: Scribner's, 1930.

Eddy, Mary Baker. *Miscellaneous Writings, 1883-1896*. Boston: Allison V. Stewart, 1910.

———. *No and Yes*. Boston: Allison V. Stewart, for the trustees under the will of Mary Baker Eddy, 1910.

———. *Rudimental Divine Science*. Boston: The trustees under the will of Mary Baker Eddy, 1908.

———. *Science and Health with Key to the Scriptures*. Boston: Allison V. Stewart, for the trustees under the will of Mary Baker Eddy. First published in 1875.

SEVENTH-DAY ADVENTISM

Martin, Walter R. *The Truth About Seventh-Day Adventism*. Grand Rapids: Zondervan, 1960.

Seventh-Day Adventists Answer Questions on Doctrine. Washington, D.C.: Review and Herald, 1957.

THEOSOPHY

Besant, Annie. *Popular Lectures on Theosophy*. Chicago: Rajput Press, 1910.

———. *Theosophy*. London and Edinburgh: T. C. & E. C. Jack, n.d.

Blavatsky, H. P. *The Key to Theosophy*. 1889. Reprint. Covina, Calif.: Theosophical University Press, 1946.

Leadbeater, C. W. *An Outline of Theosophy*. Chicago: Theosophical Book Concern, 1903.

UNITY SCHOOL OF CHRISTIANITY

Fillmore, Charles. *The Science of Being and Christian Healing*. Kansas City, Mo.: Unity Tract Society, 1920.

"I AM" MOVEMENT

The "I AM" Decrees. Los Angeles: Sindelar Studios, 1931.

King, Godfré Ray. *The "I AM" Discourses*. Chicago: St. Germain Press, 1936.

BAHA'ISM

Baha'i World Faith: Selected Writings of Baha'u'llah and Abdu'l Baha. Wilmette, Ill.: Baha'i Publishing Trust, 1956.

Effendi, Shoghi. *The Faith of Baha'u'llah*. Wilmette, Ill.: Baha'i Publishing Trust, 1959.

Esslemont, J. E. *Baha'u'llah and the New Era*. Wilmette, Ill.: Baha'i Publishing Committee, 1948.

Sohrab, Mirza Ahmad. *Broken Silence*. New York: Universal Publishing, 1942.

SWEDENBORGIANISM

Keller, Helen. *My Religion*. New York: Avon, 1927.

Life Further On. Philadelphia: American New-Church Tract and Publishing Society (booklet).

Swedenborg, Emanuel. *Emanuel Swedenborg's Works*. 21 vols. Boston and New York: Houghton Mifflin.

———. *True Christian Religion*. Boston and New York: Houghton Mifflin, 1949.

ROSICRUCIANISM

The Confederation of Initiates. Quakertown, Pa.: Fraternitatis Rosae Crucis, Dept. of Instruction, Beverly Hall.

Heindel, Max. *Rosicrucian Cosmo-Conception.* 23rd ed. London: L. N. Fowler, 1956.

The Rosicrucian Digest. San Jose, Calif. Official magazine of the Ancient Mystical Order Rosae Crucis (AMORC).

The Rosicrucian Interpretation of Christianity. Oceanside, Calif.: Rosicrucian Fellowship.

The Rosicrucian Magazine. Oceanside, Calif. Official publication of The Rosicrucian Fellowship.

The Science of Death. Oceanside, Calif.: The Rosicrucian Fellowship.

The Secret Schools. Quakertown, Pa.: Fraternitatis Rosae Crucis, Dept. of Instruction, Beverly Hall.